Praise for *F**k Work,*

'A compelling 10-step escape from corporate life that could spell a rash of resignation letters'
The Sunday Times

'Get paid to play? What a promise! But John Williams delivers. He teaches you the secrets of truly loving your work. Revolutionary!'
Suzy Walker, Editor-in-Chief, *Psychologies*

'Inspiring, actionable, and a lot of fun to read, John Williams's book takes you step by step from discovering the work you'd really enjoy doing to getting paid well for it.'
Daniel H. Pink, author of *When, Drive,* and *To Sell is Human*

'John Williams has an inspiring, actionable book that will show you how to start your own business, create your ideal job, or launch a movement to change the world.'
Nir Eyal, bestselling author of *Hooked* and *Indistractable*

'Brilliant! A much healthier and more fun approach to work that we all need now, with concrete steps to make the change. I'm gifting this to my friends that have lost the plot.'
Derek Sivers, author of *Anything You Want*

'I read the first edition of this book when it was published in 2010. John Williams was way ahead in showing readers how they could create their own businesses in small, manageable steps, based on whatever they love to do. Ten years later, I'm delighted to see that a new edition has been published. So much has changed in that time. Thanks to technology and the coronavirus pandemic, there are now yoga teachers earning more online than they ever did in a physical yoga studio. The most unlikely people now have global person brands, earning money in the most unlikely ways. *Fuck Work, Let's Play* will help you to let go of your preconceptions and social conditioning. It will show you how to turn what may seem like crazy ideas into a viable business.

John Purkiss, co-author of *Brand You* and author of *The Power of Letting Go*

'If ever there was a time to back yourself, your ideas and your ambitions, you're slap bang in the middle of that time right now. If ever there was a book proven to maximise your chances of success it's this one.'

Richard Newton, author of *The Little Book of Thinking Big*

F**k Work,
Let's Play

F**k Work, Let's Play

Do what you love and get paid for it

Second edition

JOHN WILLIAMS

Pearson

Harlow, England • London • New York • Boston • San Francisco • Toronto • Sydney
Dubai • Singapore • Hong Kong • Tokyo • Seoul • Taipei • New Delhi
Cape Town • São Paulo • Mexico City • Madrid • Amsterdam • Munich • Paris • Milan

PEARSON EDUCATION LIMITED
KAO Two
KAO Park
Harlow CM17 9SR
United Kingdom
Tel: +44 (0)1279 623623
Web: www.pearson.com/uk

First published 2010 (print)
Second edition published 2020 (print and electronic)

ISBN: 978-1-292-34936-7 (print)
       978-1-292-34937-4 (PDF)
       978-1-292-34938-1 (ePub)

British Library Cataloguing-in-Publication Data
A catalogue record for the print edition is available from the British Library

Library of Congress Cataloging-in-Publication Data
A catalog record for the print edition is available from the Library of Congress

10 9 8 7 6 5 4 3 2 1
24 23 22 21 20

Cover design by Two Associates
Print edition typeset in 10/15 Photina MT Pro by SPi Global
Printed by Ashford Colour Press Ltd, Gosport

NOTE THAT ANY PAGE CROSS REFERENCES REFER TO THE PRINT EDITION

To my father,
Edward Glyn Williams,
for five months of play

Contents

Secret ten: How to play your way to the rich life

About the author

John Williams is founder of The Ideas Lab, the company that has helped thousands of people to find something they love, get it started, and make a living out of it.

John started his career in creative technology as a developer on pioneering special effects software (including on-site work at Disney Feature Animation, LA) and broadcast automation. He became Digital Media CTO at a European start-up incubator before moving to head up a media technology consultancy team at Deloitte. He left to consult independently to the BBC and other broadcasters around the world before finally founding The Ideas Lab and writing his first best-selling book *Screw Work, Let's Play*, now translated into ten languages (and which led to this new revised and updated book).

John is also the author of *Screw Work Break Free: How to launch your own money-making idea in 30 days*, published by Vermilion. *Screw Work Break Free* goes into further detail on finding the right business or product idea to pursue and how to get it up and running in just 30 days by drawing on the latest methods of famous creatives and billion-dollar start-ups.

Read more about John, his books and The Ideas Lab at theideaslab.org

Author's acknowledgements

Nothing of any significance has ever been created by one person and this book is no exception. First, I'd like to thank Eloise Cook at Pearson for commissioning this new, updated and expanded book. Thanks also to my agent and friend Jacqueline Burns for ten years of writing adventures together.

Thanks to so many friends who have lent their support for my writing and business journey over the years: Jerry Hyde (who first suggested the title of the book should be "F**k Work"), Julian Bond, Ed Smerdon, Chris Boydell, Sam Bysh and all the members of the men's group, Richard Newton, Nicholas Leigh, Stony Grunow, Alasdair Inglis, Syrus Mokhtari, James Lawn, Liz Rivers, Candy Newman, Natasha Curnock, Julia Elmore, John Parkin, Jamie Catto, Joe Gregory and John Purkiss. And thank you to Suzy Walker for so much support over the years and to Ben Hamley for keeping The Ideas Lab running while I was writing.

Thanks to the business mentors who I have learned from or partnered with: Rob Tyson, Judith Morgan, Barbara Sher, Nick Williams, Daniel Wagner, Mark Forster, Barbara Winter and Nina Grunfeld. Thanks to Richard Alderson and the team at Careershifters who helped me get started so many years ago.

Thanks to Wolfgang Wild for introducing me to Pearson a decade ago and to Samantha Jackson for her involvement in the original edition of this book. A debt also to the authors whose books I have been inspired by – Pat Kane, Seth Godin, Dan Pink and Jeetendr Sehdev.

Lots of love to my mum Diane Williams for teaching me that play is just as important as work and who still has plenty of play projects on the go. And to my brother David for his entrepreneurial outlook and for first coaching me on how to customise a job. And thank you to the three generations of scientists, engineers and entrepreneurs who went before me. I hope I've done you proud.

Thank you to all my clients who have bravely shared the dreams and challenges of their working lives with me.

Thanks to my busy interview subjects who were kind enough to give their time in aid of this book: Sam Bompas and Harry Parr of Bompas & Parr; Sophie Boss of Beyond Chocolate; Petra Barran of Kerb Food; David Crane of Smoke Free App; Adam Wilder of Togetherness; Charlie & Harry Thuillier of Oppo Ice Cream; Tim Smit, creator of the Eden Project; Leslie Scott, creator of Jenga; Derek Sivers, founder of CD Baby; editor of *The Idler*, Tom Hodgkinson; Ernesto Moreno of Arepa & co; David Pearl; Jody Day of Gateway Women; Damian Barr of The Literary Salon; Sarah Weiler of Power of Uke; and Dan Barker.

And finally to you for reading this book. I hope you'll go out and recruit more people to the play cause. You can find all my social media links and how to contact me at fworkletsplay.com or tweet me to say hello on @johnsw

Publisher's acknowledgements

Text credits

1 **Charles Handy:** Quoted by Charles Handy 2 **Derek Sivers:** Quoted by Derek Sivers 2 **Pat Kane:** Quoted by Pat Kane 4 **Brian Sutton-Smith:** Quoted by Brian Sutton-Smith 6 **Richard Branson:** Quotes by Sir Richard Branson 6 **Steve Jobs:** Quoted by Steve Jobs 7 **Sonja Lyubomirsky:** Quoted by Sonja Lyubomirsky 7 **Ken Robinson:** Quoted by Sir Ken Robinson 11 **Taylor Croonquist/Camille Holden:** Taylor Croonquist and Camille Holden 13 **Pat Kane:** Quoted by Pat Kane 15 **Nagle Jackson:** Quoted by Nagle Jackson 18 **Sussex Publishers:** Peter Gray Ph.D., "Play Makes Us Human V: Why Hunter-Gatherers' Work is Play Hunter-gatherers made work play by making it optional". Psychology Today, Jul 02, 2009 18 **Joseph Campbell:** Quoted by Joseph Campbell 19 **Jeff Bezos:** Quoted by Jeff Bezos 19 **Indra Nooyi:** Quoted by Indra Nooyi 24 **Mae West:** Quoted by Mae West 24 **Petra Barran:** Petra Barran 26 **Robert Fritz:** Quoted by Robert Fritz 28 **Richard Branson:** Quoted by Richard Branson 30 **Petra Barran:** Petra Barran 34 **Brian Eno:** Quoted by Brian Eno 38 **Sarah Weiler:** Sarah Weiler 48 **Abraham Maslow:** Quoted by Abraham Maslow 52 **Aristotle:** Quoted by Aristotle 52 **The McEvoy Group, LLC:** The Beatles anthology. (2000). San Francisco: Chronicle Books. 58 **BELBIN Associates:** Belbin. (2012). Team Roles at Work. doi: 10.4324/9780080963242 63 **Charlie Thuillier:** Quoted by Charlie Thuillier 64 **Abraham Maslow:** Quoted by Abraham Maslow 68 **Ernesto Moreno:** Quoted by Ernesto Moreno 70 **Carl Rogers:** Quoted by Carl Rogers 77 **Dame Anita Roddick:** Quoted by Dame Anita Roddick 77 **Harry Parr:** Harry Parr 79 **Sam Bompas:** Sam Bompas

80 Warren Buffett: Quoted by Warren Buffett **82 Eckhart Tolle:** Quoted by Eckhart Tolle **83 Penguin Random House:** Sonja Lyubomirsky (2007), "The How of Happiness: A New Approach to Getting the Life You Want", Penguin. **84 Penguin Random House:** Sonja Lyubomirsky (2007), "The How of Happiness: A New Approach to Getting the Life You Want", Penguin. **89 Sam Bompas:** Sam Bompas **93 Matt Mullenweg:** Quoted by Matt Mullenweg **94 Liz Smith:** Quoted by Liz Smith **95 Henry David Thoreau:** Quoted by Henry David Thoreau **100 Abraham Maslow:** Quoted by Abraham Maslow **100 Harry Thuillier:** Quoted by Harry Thuillier **101 Charlie Thuillier:** Charlie Thuillier **107 Pete Cohen:** Quoted by Pete Cohen **110 Barbara Sher:** Quoted by Barbara Sher **112 Anais Nin:** Quoted by Anais Nin **114 Dag Hammarskjöld:** Quoted by Dag Hammarskjöld **116 Derek Sivers:** Quoted by Derek Sivers **127 Buckminster Fuller:** Quoted by Buckminster Fuller **127 Pablo Picasso:** Quoted by Pablo Picasso **128 John Dewey:** Quoted by John Dewey **128 Linus Pauling:** Quoted by Linus Pauling **129 Tom Hodgkinson:** Quoted by Tom Hodgkinson, (2007) **130 Benjamin Franklin:** Quoted by Benjamin Franklin **130 J.K. Rowling:** Quoted by J.K. Rowling **130 James D. Watson:** Quoted by James D. Watson **131 Winston Churchill:** Quoted by Winston Churchill **131 Winston Churchill:** Quoted by Winston Churchill **133 Harv Eker:** Quoted by T. Harv Eker **134 David Crane:** David Crane **139 Hachette Livre:** Sophie Boss, Audrey Boss, (2012) "Beyond Chocolate: The mindful way to a healthy relationship with food and your body" Hachette UK **149 Sophia Loren:** Quoted by Sophia Loren **149 The New York Times Company:** Bee Shapiro, A Shortcut to Comic CelebrityBee Shapiro, The New York Times, Sept. 17, 2014 **150 THE FINANCIAL TIMES LTD:** John Sunyer, Lunch with the FT: The Fat Jew, Financial Times, JULY 24 2015 **150 Josh Ostrovsky:** Quoted by Josh Ostrovsky **156 Robert Stephens:** Quoted by Robert Stephens **157 Elon Musk:** Quoted by Elon Musk **158 Stuart Wilde:** Quoted by Stuart Wilde **158 Seth Godin:** Quoted by Seth Godin

159 **David Pearl:** David Pearl **173 Jeetendr Sehdev:** Quoted by Jeetendr Sehdev **175 Abraham Maslow:** Quoted by Abraham Maslow **175 Ray Charles:** Quoted by Ray Charles **178 Charles Handy:** Quoted by Charles Handy **178 Adam Wilder:** Adam Wilder **180 Theodore Levitt:** Theodore Levitt, Harvard Business School marketing professor **195 Sarah Caldwell:** Quoted by Sarah Caldwell **195 Dan Barker:** Dan Barker **197 Eddie Izzard:** Quoted by Eddie Izzard **210 Thomas Edison:** Quoted by Thomas Edison **210 Derek Sivers:** Derek Sivers **211 Seth Godin:** Quoted by Seth Godin **212 Leslie Scott:** Leslie Scott **217 Jay-Z:** Quoted by Jay-Z **220 Damian Barr:** Quoted by Damian Barr **221 Judith Morgan:** Quoted by Judith Morgan **229 Zig Ziglar:** Quoted by Zig Ziglar **229 Leslie Scott:** Quoted by Leslie Scott **230 Elon Musk:** Quoted by Elon Musk **230 Anita Roddick:** Quoted by Anita Roddick **231 Richard Bandler:** Quoted by Richard Bandler **234 Tom Hodgkinson:** Quoted by Tom Hodgkinson **235 Petra Barran:** Petra Barran **235 Henry David Thoreau:** Quoted by Henry David Thoreau **238 Jim Rohn:** Quoted by Jim Rohn **248 Sophie Boss:** Sophie Boss

Photo credit

Inside cover image Saskia Nelson: Photographed by Saskia Nelson

About this book (and why 'F**k Work'?)

This book will show you step by step how to get paid to play by turning the things you love doing into a living. Whether you're currently feeling trapped in a job you don't enjoy or you're slogging away at your own business that's never quite taken off, you'll find both the life-changing concepts and the practical strategies you need to transform your working life.

This is not about just having fun and hoping the money will magically fall out of the sky. I will show you the key to getting paid for doing what feels like play to you (regardless of the state of the economy), how to win your first 'paycheque', and then how to scale it up to making a living – and maybe even get rich (whatever that means for you). And if you still have no idea what you want to do with your life, I'll show you how to get clear on that first.

Whether you want to launch your own business, take your work online, get into consulting, become a digital nomad, create your ideal job from scratch, write a bestseller, get famous for your creative work, make millions, or change the world, this book will help you. I can't show you how to "get rich quick". I haven't found anything yet that does that (let me know if you do). If anything, it's about how to get *happy* quick. The fact is, whatever you want your life to be, you can create some taste of your ideal right now in the present. Doing this will make you happier and, as you will see, happiness helps you get to success and wealth.

A new book for a new decade

Ten years ago, I could see multiple factors converging to change the world of work forever – automation, outsourcing, the global marketplace for skills, and a thousand free and affordable online tools to enable us to start something we love, get known and get paid for. But it seemed that much of this had not entered the daily conversation in the media and in conventional careers and business advice. This is why I wrote *Screw Work, Let's Play*, the original incarnation of this book. It was a cult hit and was featured in *The Sunday Times*, *The Times*, *The Financial Times*, and many other newspapers and magazines. It has since been translated into ten languages.

Now, ten years later, the ideas in that book are ready for the mainstream. So many more of us could be getting paid to play if we only had access to the strategies to do so. *Screw Work, Let's Play* was written in the aftermath of the banking crisis. When I started this new edition of the book the world was once again in a period of some political and economic uncertainty – and then the coronavirus pandemic hit us. Millions lost their jobs. Many were furloughed. More people than ever have been reassessing their work and realising that they need to take charge of their own careers.

Whatever the state of the world is at the point you are reading this, I guarantee that you will be better off leaving behind the fixed thinking of the obedient worker and adopting the creative and entrepreneurial approach of the 'player' laid out here.

The principles of the original book have never been more relevant, but it was in need of an update. Online marketing and social media in particular have changed dramatically. And the stories of some of the people I interviewed have moved on in remarkable ways.

So it's time for a new edition of the book. And for a new title too. When I was wrestling with what to call my first book a creative mentor of mine said "This is a book with a strong and important message; surely it's got to be 'Fuck Work'?" In the end I pulled my punches a little by choosing *Screw Work, Let's Play*.

Today I know that everything I wrote about has not only been shown to be true but even more relevant than it was then. And we have a hundred times the opportunities now for making a living doing something we love. Plus when I got in touch with some of the people I'd interviewed for the original book for an update, I found that they had grown their early playful projects into incredibly cool international businesses using exactly the kind of creative approaches I had written about. So it's time for a title as strong as the message – *F**k Work, Let's Play!*

What you're holding in your hands now is a new, updated and expanded book. There are updates and additions to the advice, remarkable updates to the entrepreneurial stories, complete new case studies, countless tweaks and improvements, and new advice from my experience of the last ten years helping people get paid to play in the form of 'Power-Ups'. Those are strategies to sidestep the pitfalls I've seen many fall into and accelerate your journey to getting paid to play.

Here's how the book works.

The ten secrets

The book is arranged as ten secrets to getting paid to play. These are not secrets that anyone is wilfully withholding from you and yet it's remarkable how few of us know them. We're certainly not taught them in school or college. They sometimes run counter to commonly held wisdom we hear every day and, until you know them, you are likely to be trapped forever in unsatisfying work.

The secrets are arranged in sequence to take you all the way from having no idea what work you would enjoy to making a full-time living doing something you love. It's therefore best to read each Secret in sequence as each one builds on the last.

This is what you will discover in each Secret.

Secret one: How to work out what you really really want

If you know you want to do something different but can't for the life of you work out what it is, this will finally help you. And if you're already on the way to doing what you want, don't skip this Secret because it will show just how important choosing the right work is to becoming a success.

Secret two: How to choose what to do next

How to find the sweet spot between what you love doing and what people will pay for. How to choose which avenue to pursue even when you feel completely stuck – either because you have no idea what you want or because you have so many ideas you can't make up your mind. Oh, and the scientifically proven formula for happiness.

Secret three: How to get started right now

How to escape the trap of endless research and get started right away on your new life. Why you don't need elaborate plans or even necessarily to set goals. How to start even the grandest project in a scaled-down form without quitting your current work.

Secret four: How to guarantee your success

It can be a rocky ride on the way to getting paid to play. Read this Secret to find out how you can become indestructible and guarantee you can make it whatever may happen along the way.

Secret five: How to play for profit and purpose

Worried that doing what you really enjoy will land you in poverty? This Secret will show you how to do things that are fun for you in a way that provides real value to people – and so get paid for it.

Secret six: How to play the fame game and win

How to get known, or even famous, for what you do so that you attract the opportunities you want. How to use digital marketing and social media to help you launch yourself on to the world at little or no cost.

Secret seven: How to create an irresistible offer

How to offer something people really want and choose the best way to deliver it, from selling a service to creating something online that makes you money while you sleep.

Secret eight: How to win your first paycheque

How to earn your very first piece of income for something that feels like play to you – without having to quit your current work.

Secret nine: How to play full time

How to scale up your first experiments to something you can get paid for full time whether in self-employment, your own business, a portfolio career, or in what I call 'Job 2.0' – the customised job. Plus, how to make it happen quicker than you might expect.

Secret ten: How to play your way to the rich life

This Secret will show you how to get clear what a rich life looks like to you. Is it financial riches, the freedom to travel the planet, having plenty of free time, or the power to change the world? Discover the five keys to get you there including the PRICE strategy to charge what you're really worth.

The 21 myths of work

I've worked with thousands of clients over the past 15 years, and over and over again I see the same mistaken beliefs that stop people from doing what they want. These are often beliefs inherited from a previous generation that had far fewer choices about their work than we do now. I've boiled these down to 21 myths. You'll find them peppered throughout the book and you will see each one being dismantled. You can also read the full list at the end of the book. How many of them are you currently holding as the truth? They may well be what's holding you back. Are you ready to open your mind to some new ideas about work?

I think of the 21 myths like this: imagine an old prop plane sitting on the runway with its engine running. If you release the brakes and remove the chocks, it's inevitable that it's going to start rolling – but you're still going to need to apply some gas in order to take off. If I can just take away all the myths you believe about work, it is inevitable you will start moving towards what you want. Of course, you'll still need to apply some gas to take flight and get where you want to go.

Expert interviews

I've met many successful 'players' through my work running The Ideas Lab and you can read their advice and stories throughout this book. Some of them have created, run and sold million-pound businesses. Some are clients I've helped start from nothing and some are shining examples of the new possibilities of work that I've met through my events and The Ideas Lab podcast.

Some interviewees are very wealthy, while others are living on a more modest income but have succeeded in structuring their lives around freedom, creativity and variety. Some are on a mission to change the world. They are all living rich lives in the broadest sense of the word.

You can listen to or watch many of the full interviews with the players at fworkletsplaycom.

The website

Throughout the book and at the end of each Secret, I have pointed you to further information, tools and resources on the accompanying minisite: fworkletsplay.com Go there now to listen to and watch interviews, download worksheets and read updates to the book as they become available.

Join the play revolution

For the first time in the human experience, we have a chance to shape our work to suit the way we live instead of our lives to fit our work . . . We would be mad to miss the chance.

Charles Handy, management expert and author

We're lucky. We've reached a remarkable point in the history of work. Today, it's possible to make a living out of pretty much anything. In fact, scratch that, you can make a living out of *absolutely* anything. Seriously, whatever you can think of, someone somewhere in the world is making a career of it.

During the course of my research for this book I've met remarkable examples like Sam Bompas and Harry Parr, who turned their quirky food experiments in architectural jellies and breathable cocktails into an international flavour studio; Adam Wilder who creates unique experiences from silent dating to breaking the world record for the number of people spooning; Petra Barran who grew her love for street food into an organisation that changed food culture forever; David Crane who used his passion for psychology to create the world's #1 stop smoking app.

These people are part of a growing tribe around the world who are not content just to make a wage to pay the rent, but want their lives to be about something larger. Creating something unique, saying something important, trying new experiences, having some fun, taking a few risks, and daring to fall flat on their faces – or win big and strike it rich. They want freedom, variety, challenge and excitement. They want to stretch themselves, and to keep evolving every day.

What we're witnessing is no less than a revolution in what work can be. The word 'job' is irrelevant. Even the word 'work' seems a poor choice for the lifestyles this new tribe have crafted for themselves. Musician turned entrepreneur, Derek Sivers, who sold his business for $22 million says, "This isn't work, it's play."

Our vocabulary is out of date. You could call some of these people entrepreneurs or business people, but the old image of someone dressed in a sober suit spouting management speak just doesn't fit. The player's uniform is just as likely to be jeans and T-Shirt or, for those working at home, pyjamas.

Previous generations had little choice about their working lives. A job for life was standard, and the alternative of starting a business often required expensive premises, a team of staff and huge advertising costs. The business world was littered with gatekeepers who got to choose who could come in based on background, race, gender or any other arbitrary parameter. Now, no one can stop you crafting your work life exactly as you would like it.

The internet and mobile technology have freed us all to work however, wherever, whenever we want. Old restrictive boundaries are dissolving between local and global, employee and entrepreneur, professional and amateur, consumer and producer, home and office, work and play. Our options are now so much broader than just employee or business owner. What does all this mean? It means that there really is no reason left to suffer boring, unfulfilling work.

We no longer need to be driven by the old work ethic. We have entered the era of what author Pat Kane calls 'The Play Ethic'.

This is 'play' as the great philosophers understood it: the experience of being an active, creative and fully autonomous person. The play ethic is about having the confidence to be spontaneous, creative and empathetic across every area of your life . . . It's about placing yourself, your passions and enthusiasms at the centre of your world.

Pat Kane, author of *The Play Ethic: A Manifesto for a Different Way of Living*, taken from www.theplayethic.com

Does 'play' sound selfish to you? It's actually the opposite. Players are often as interested in what they can give to the world as what they can get from it. Outdoor clothing company Patagonia grew out of a passion for rock climbing but is now worth a billion dollars. The company is an outspoken defender of the environment, repairs their clothing for free, and donated their recent $10 million tax cut from the US government to groups committed to environmental causes.

Online eyewear retailer Warby Parker arose out of an idea formed between business school students in a bar. The company is now valued at $1.75 billion and they provide a free pair of glasses to someone in need in the developing world for every pair of Warby Parker glasses purchased. The company has now distributed more than 5 million pairs of free glasses.

Campaigner Tristram Stuart fed 5,000 people in London's Trafalgar Square from misshapen food that would normally go to waste. Now he's created beer brand Toast to make use of the 44% of bread that is thrown away every day. Toast Ale is an award-winning beer brewed with unsold bread from bakeries and sandwich-makers. And Toast Ale gives 100% of its profits to Feed-back, an environmental charity campaigning to end food waste.

So are you ready to play? Perhaps you're currently stuck in a job that's reducing you to tears. Or you're worried that your job is under threat. Or you're slogging away at a business that's never quite taken off. In all likelihood you've been doing a lot of thinking about this, going round and round in circles trying to discover the way out. Well, it's time to end all that. Let's begin your transformation from worker to player. This book will show you the way: how to have fun and get paid for it; how to design a life big enough to hold everything that you are; how to explore and indulge your every interest; how to embrace a new world of uncertainty and enjoy the ride; how to get the results you never dared dream of with a lot less struggle; and how to stop waiting and get started on all this right now.

Join the revolution

It is my opinion that the 21st century will be the century of play.

Brian Sutton-Smith, Professor Emeritus of Education at the
University of Pennsylvania and prominent play theorist

American author Daniel Pink is a leading thinker on the changing world of work. In his classic book *A Whole New Mind* he suggests we have reached a new era requiring very different skills if we want to stay in the game. Back in the 19th century, the industrial revolution gave us massive factories and efficient assembly lines. The factory worker needed physical strength and manual skills to thrive. The 20th century ushered in the information age with the knowledge worker who needed analytical and logical skills. Today in the 21st century we find ourselves in the Conceptual Age.

The skills we need now, Pink says, are what you might call right-brain functions (even if that isn't neurologically accurate) such as design, empathy, meaning and play. Those of us showing inventiveness, empathy and big picture capabilities – players – will be the ones to excel. The industrial revolution, paired with the Protestant work ethic, gave us the *worker*. Today's digital revolution has given us the *player*.

This is not a shift you can sit back and opt out of. Logical information age skills are still necessary but they will no longer be sufficient. Work that can be easily defined and reproduced is likely to be either automated or outsourced. New forms of automation are now affecting this generation's white-collar workers in similar ways as it did the last generation's blue-collar workers.

According to a 2019 Brookings Institution report, a quarter of jobs in the US alone will be severely disrupted by AI and automation. And in a 2018 PwC survey of 10,029 people in China, Germany, India, the UK and the US, 37% said they were worried

4   F**K WORK, LET'S PLAY

about the impact of automation on jobs. AI alone is expected to have a $15.7 trillion economic impact by 2030.

While this disruption has started with less skilled roles like shop workers, drivers and clerical roles, it has started to impact those in sales, customer service, IT, science and engineering, healthcare and law. As an example, law firms are already using AI to perform due diligence, conduct research and bill hours, and it's predicted AI will eliminate most paralegal and legal research positions within the next decade. To survive, you must develop skills that computers can't do better, faster, or cheaper.

What can't be automated may be outsourced to equally capable but cheaper staff in other countries. This has already extended from IT to financial analysis, editorial work and completing tax returns.

But the economy!

Just as I was finishing this book, the coronavirus pandemic hit us and most of the world went into lockdown. Some experts are now predicting a deep recession. Other experts are predicting a boom as we are allowed out of our homes again.

Whatever the state of the world at the point you are reading this, don't be one of those that use the economy as an excuse to put off making a change. Too many people tell me they're not thinking about their career right now because there's a recession on (or on the way) so they should just keep their head down, stay put and play safe.

Burying your head in the sand is the last thing you should be doing in a time of change and uncertainty. Firstly, it's in times of flux that you are most likely to lose your job. If your boss calls you in this Friday and says it's your last day, wouldn't you rather have done the thinking already on what to do next than have to rush to start from scratch the following Monday? Secondly, the people who survive setbacks and crises the best are those who bring the kind of creative thinking you'll be learning over the next few chapters. Thirdly, when you create a business that is entirely under your control you can quickly adapt to whatever the world throws at you. Finally, it's in the times of greatest change that the most exciting opportunities emerge. More people became millionaires during the Great Depression than in any other time in American history because start-up costs are so much lower in a downturn.

This book will show you how to test out your new line of work without quitting what you do now so that by the time you do leave you know you can generate income. And if you're reading this book because you've been made redundant, don't waste this chance to rethink your work and move towards play.

It pays to have fun

I never went into business to make money – but I have found that, if I have fun, the money will come.

Sir Richard Branson, founder of Virgin

Having fun is at the heart of the idea of playing. And fun makes good financial sense too. The world's richest and most successful people, including billionaires Richard Branson, Warren Buffett and Oprah Winfrey, say they do what they do because it's fun. They clearly don't continue working because they need the money.

Apple's Steve Jobs famously advised the following:

Your work is going to fill a large part of your life, and the only way to be truly satisfied is to do what you believe is great work. And the only way to do great work is to love what you do. If you haven't found it yet, keep looking. Don't settle.

If you're currently chasing success and money in an attempt to make yourself happy you may have got things the wrong way round. Research by Professor Sonja Lyubomirsky of the University of California revealed that happiness, in many cases, leads to successful outcomes, rather than merely following from them.

After reviewing 225 relevant studies, her results show that happier people are more creative and productive, more likely to attempt new challenges, and to push themselves to strive for fresh goals. They are also more likely to be liked by their peers, and thus recruited to better jobs and promoted to higher positions. As a result of all this, happy people accrue more money.

So how do we become happier? Choosing the right work is a good start. The evidence demonstrates that people who have jobs distinguished by autonomy, meaning and variety are significantly happier than those who don't. As the good professor explains:

> *When it comes to work life, we can create our own so-called 'upward spirals'. The more successful we are at our jobs, the higher income we make, and the better work environment we have, the happier we will be. This increased happiness will foster greater success, more money, and an improved work environment, which will further enhance happiness, and so on and so on and so on.*

This book will show you how to begin this upward spiral by choosing the right work and by creating a happier, more enjoyable life in the present.

> *When you find yourself in love with something you're good at, you never really work again.*
>
> **Sir Ken Robinson, British author and expert on creativity and education**

The key to getting paid for playing is to choose the right things to play. And the right things are those that you are naturally good at. Your aim must be to get into 'flow' – building a working life around the things you enjoy doing and have a natural talent for. But to do this, you need to widen your perception of what constitutes a talent far beyond the limited concept of 'transferable skills'.

It's important to understand the distinction between talent and skill. Talent appears early in life. Using our talents feels good so we do it a lot. Skill comes later as a result of practising that talent. We are musical before we ever pick up an instrument. People who are great communicators have usually been chatting to anyone who would listen since they formed their first words. Writers often start reading early. Great salespeople have been influencing and negotiating since they started school. Success is so much easier and more enjoyable when we build our work around our natural talents and developed skills.

So if we understand this, why aren't we all getting paid to have fun? First, a lot of people are simply doing the wrong work. Most of us have made gross compromises in our choice of work, driven by the principles of a previous generation who didn't have the options we do today. We have never dared to be selective enough about what we do so that we can spend the majority of the time in flow. As a result, we haven't mined that rich seam of gold among the masses of grey rock.

Some people think it's nonsense to make a living out of what you love because they've never experienced it. The school system sets us up for this when it encourages us to work on our weaknesses. But you'd be better off to work on your strengths and work *around* your weaknesses.

Of course, in a conventional job it can be difficult to say 'I don't do presentations, I only do research' or 'I don't do research, I only do presentations'. We're supposed to be great all-rounders – good at being creative, organising our time, working in a team, creating thorough reports, presenting our findings, and dotting the Is and crossing the Ts. In reality, no one can excel at all these things, and trying to do so guarantees mediocrity. The result is that work becomes a struggle and we lose sight of just how talented we are.

When you finally work *with* your personality and strengths, and avoid the ill-fitting work that drags you down, the effect is like dropping into a jetstream. You will see not just an incremental improvement in your results but a dramatic multiplication.

This is one reason why people are increasingly attracted to various forms of self-employment.

Get the autonomy you crave

Given the limitations of conventional jobs, it's not surprising so many people would like an alternative. More people than ever are going self-employed – in the US it's a third of the entire workforce. And studies place the number wanting to move into self-employment as high as 70%. Too many are still held back by the myths of what it takes to work for yourself (we'll be dismantling every one of these myths later in the book).

A common belief is that the natural alternative to a job is to launch a business with all the risk and complexities of premises, staff and funding. But there are now so many different ways to make an income without a job. These constitute a third way – between jobs and the traditional business – and include consulting, freelancing, online business, portfolio career, and creating a personal brand around your expertise.

The line between employed and self-employed is blurred and it is no longer necessary to jump straight from one to another. Now we can test out our ideas, prove that they work and earn our first playcheque before we quit – or we can just keep it as a nice sideline to our employment. We can even reinvent the humble job to create the 'customised job', moulded to suit our personality, and our preferred working structure and location.

Whatever its form, the difference is primarily one of attitude. It's a shift in responsibility from passive employee to active creator.

It's a 180-degree about-turn, from looking outward for someone else to define our work to looking inward and creating the working life we really want. This is the shift from worker to player.

We are in a new era of work. The industrial revolution gave us mass production – treating employees as interchangeable components in a machine, creating generic products, and selling them to a mass market of undifferentiated consumers. Nearly two centuries later, today's digital revolution is changing the face of work all over again, but this time it's about a shift towards individuals and micro-businesses creating innovative products for niche markets, and attracting fans who market the products they like to each other.

The world is your office

Thanks to laptop computers, mobile phones and WiFi, we are now freed from the tyranny of the office cubicle. A 2017 Gallup survey of 15,000 adults found that 43% of employed Americans, for instance, already spend at least some time working remotely. The pandemic has massively accelerated this shift with millions realising they can work at home just as effectively (or perhaps more) than at the office,

If your work is portable, you are free to choose where you work and who with. Join the new mobile workers now found in parks, cafés and even sitting beside the swimming pool in exotic locations. According to 2019 research by MBO Partners, 16 million Americans plan on working as 'digital nomads' over the next two to three years, while another 41 million Americans are considering it.

If you want freedom without losing a sense of community, you can become a member of one of the 15,000+ shared workspaces around the world that provide desk space by the hour, day or month. The original version of this book was mostly written in a workspace for social entrepreneurs called Impact Hub. Now with over 100 branches in 50 countries, it's a workspace, meeting space, café and social community. The members are people who want to build businesses and organisations where making a difference is as important as making a profit. Similar spaces are appearing for artists, media professionals and tech start-ups.

Once you're free of the office, the next step is to realise that you may also be free of the country you live in. Here's how one couple transitioned to being digital nomads.

Speed-dating cities

Taylor Croonquist and Camille Holden live in Bali where they run Nuts & Bolts Speed Training, providing advanced online training courses for PowerPoint users. I met Taylor in Ubud, Bali, and he told me the story of how they found their favourite place to live while setting up the business:

> We were living in China when we quit our jobs six years ago. And we wanted to find the next best place to live in the world because we thought China was the best place until the pollution went off the charts. We came up with this idea that we should speed-date cities around the world for two years, spending two to three months in each city so we could get a feel for the place and the people. And then to finance that we decided to launch this venture creating and selling online training courses. In the beginning it was pretty low key. We weren't trying make it a career, just make enough to buy aeroplane tickets and food and housing. We thought we could find enough clients along the way who we can teach PowerPoint to fund ourselves.
>
> Because we weren't making any money at the beginning we started searching house-sitting and pet-sitting websites and we

lucked out with a two-month house-sitting gig by the beach in Fiji. That's where we built and launched our website and started selling our first online training course.

We stayed in nine places over the next couple of years. One highlight was Jimena de la Frontera in Spain. It had a nice small town feel but we felt it would be too small for us in the long term. Kiev was at the other end of the scale and was a wonderful surprise. The food was amazing, the people were really friendly, and for $800 a month we were able to rent a big apartment in one of the swankiest neighbourhoods that had all of the best restaurants and activities.

After two years of traveling and running our business we were covering our costs plus saving a little bit of money, so we said let's do a third year. The business got even better but we wanted to stop moving at that point so we didn't have to keep living out of our suitcase.

We started asking travellers out of all the places they had been where would they move back to for six months? Where would they be super happy? And after the fourth pretty cool couple said they'd move back to Ubud, Bali, in a heartbeat we decided to just give it a shot and bought one-way tickets. We thought, worst case, if we don't like it two months in, we'll just go somewhere else. In fact, we never left.

We've been here in Bali for three years now. And it's about six years since we had the idea to travel around the world and find a way to finance it. The biggest learning curve for us was learning how to market our products online and how to create a website that generates traffic on its own. Last year, we had 1.5 million visitors to our website, and we are now getting about 200,000 visitors a month, so we are still growing. Today, Nuts and Bolts Speed Training is our full-time gig that we can take anywhere in the world with us.

Find out more about Taylor & Camille's business at
nutsandboltsspeedtraining.com

Now that the world is your office, you can live and work wherever you choose. Where would you like to go?

I now base myself in East London with occasional one or two month-long trips to Asia. This new edition of the book you are holding in your hands was written on the island of Koh Lanta in Thailand between cafés on the beach and a friendly co-working space called KoHub.

You'll find more advice on how to become a digital nomad in Secret ten.

From worker to player

To call yourself a 'player', rather than a 'worker', is to immediately widen your conception of who you are and what you might be capable of doing. It is to dedicate yourself to realising your full human potential; to be active, not passive.

Pat Kane, ThePlayEthic.com

What we're seeing is a new generation of people with a very different attitude to work. They are not workers but players. What exactly does that mean? Here are nine traits of players that this book will help you to understand and adopt.

1. Players put creativity, fun and fulfilment first

The worker expects work to be a chore. As players, we place what really matters to us at the centre of our worlds and we fill our lives with whatever we find most exciting, enjoyable, challenging, rewarding and fulfilling. We want to indulge every aspect of ourselves. We want to play all day and get paid for it. The player's ultimate career goal is often 'to get paid for being me'.

2. Players are multifaceted

Workers take a restricted version of themselves to the office, putting on a mask for the corporate environment. Players bring all of themselves. Players are not one-dimensional beings (no human being is). Players are musicians who are also start-up founders, travellers who are also bloggers, consultants who are also songwriters, comedians who are also psychotherapists, finance administrators who are also campaigners. Now we can be all of who we are.

3. Players respond to the world around them

The worker thinks that play is frittering away time. But playing isn't about sitting in a corner all day daydreaming, nor is it sitting on a beach drinking cocktails for the rest of your life (that's the dream of a worker not a player). Look at what children do when they play – they are interacting with the physical world around them, testing it and experimenting with it, and they are also interacting with others and learning about relationships. Play is exploratory and responsive. To be *in play* is to be actively engaged in the world.

A player therefore is not ignoring the real world – far from it. We are being more responsive than the worker who simply does what they're told or the business owner who follows whatever money-making strategy the latest expert recommends. Players make their lives a laboratory and learn from their own experience.

4. Players respond to their inner world

The worker is directed by external expectations and values. As players, we recognise what is happening inside of us, accept it, acknowledge it and use it – long before others are even aware of it. The musician, music producer and artist Brian Eno said that the question that has occupied much of his life is 'What is it I really like?' By accepting what he discovers years before it is fashionable to do so, he has become a thought leader who created an entire genre of music (now known as ambient). He has gone on to work with some of the biggest bands in the world including U2 and Coldplay.

5. Players are mavericks

Workers stick to the conventions of their industry or specialism. As players we indulge all our interests no matter how whimsical or disparate they may seem – sometimes resulting in misunderstanding and ridicule from others. And later we emerge with genre-smashing creative works and rule-breaking businesses. Players change the game for everyone else.

The truly great advances of this generation will be made by those who can make outrageous connections, and only a mind which knows how to play can do that.

Nagle Jackson, theatre director and award-winning playwright

Players don't know when to stop. We get obsessive about things that others barely notice. We follow paths that lead us through seemingly unrelated topics and sometimes end up in some controversial area of art, politics or religion. In our free exploration we tread on others' taboos. We are broader than most, more whole. We are political beings, emotional beings, sexual beings and we know how to employ all of what we are to the greatest effect.

6. Players never stop exploring, never stop learning

When children play, there is often no predetermined outcome in mind: they are simply going where they are drawn in the moment. The play maps the growing edge of their human organism. Tomorrow's play will never be exactly the same as today. And then we reach adulthood and most people just stop.

The worker will attend the standard company training programmes and learn some new skills for their job but they rarely re-enter that process of following their growing edge wherever it leads them. Players, however, remain ever curious and are hungry to learn new things. We are still willing to experiment and follow the drive in us to expand. We're engaged in a lifelong process of learning and exploring.

Many of us are 'scanners', as careers expert Barbara Sher would call us, always moving on to the next new thing. We go where we feel instinctively drawn rather than following conventional rules of success and wealth. And that path leads to true originality. In a time of information overload, we add to the signal, not to the noise.

7. Players are not naive

Players are not new-age dreamers. We play with capitalism, we notice what our market needs and we see providing value and making money as part of the game. Players understand that money makes play sustainable. And players often make *more* money than workers because we love what we do (and that passion is attractive), we are thought leaders creating original solutions, we focus on creating genuine value (not just making a quick buck), and we solve real-world problems.

8. Players surf the big waves that others are drowned by

We need to be responsive, flexible and playful today because the world is changing so fast. Whether it's political shifts, economic shocks or unexpected crises like the global pandemic, the world seems a less stable place than it once was. At the time of writing, the global economy is more uncertain than at any time in the last decade. And this is on top of a longer-term shift of economic dominance from North America and Western Europe to Asia as China is set to soon become the world's largest economy (and India's economy is on track to beat even China's by 2030).

As the next wave of outsourcing takes away any work that is easily defined and repeated, creativity will be the safest pursuit as it is specific to the local culture and environment. Now, more than ever, everything is in play and only the playful will survive.

9. Players understand that play is not effortless

Surely there's always work required to create a successful life? Well, I have a problem with the word 'work'. There are multiple meanings for the word. One meaning refers to paid employment and it's associated with that old two-state way of living between doing the things you get paid for and doing what you really enjoy in the stolen moments outside office hours. This is why we need some new vocabulary.

Another meaning of work, however, is simply the 'exertion of effort' which is still very much relevant. Play after all is not effortless: just watch a football match, U2 playing live, or a child building a sandcastle. Even playing a video game requires attention, concentration and persistence.

Players are engaged in something larger than the word 'work' can represent. They're creating businesses around their passion, pursuing creative and artistic experiments, starting their own social movements. They're exploring the world, what they enjoy and what they can do. They are seeking the fullest expression of themselves. They're so passionate about what they're doing, they can't stop talking about it. What's work and what's leisure blur into one. It's all a form of play.

Take a tip from the hunter-gatherers

For all of modern society's sophistication, we could still learn something from the hunter-gatherer tribes remaining in remote locations around the world. Peter Gray is a research professor of psychology at Boston College who has studied the research on hunter-gatherer cultures. He has concluded that they do not have our concept of work as a compulsory chore. He writes on psychologytoday.com that hunter-gatherers' work is simply an extension of children's play.

> Children play at hunting, gathering, hut construction, tool making, meal preparations, defense against predators, birthing, infant care, healing, negotiation, and so on and so on; and gradually, as their play becomes increasingly skilled, the activities become productive. The play becomes work, but it does not cease being play. It may even become more fun than before, because the productive quality helps the whole band and is valued by all.

And work is always a choice:

> They deliberately avoid telling each other how to behave, in work as in any other context. [Despite this] long-term shirking apparently happens rarely if at all. It is exciting to go out hunting or gathering with the others, and it would be boring to stay in camp day after day. The fact that on any given day the work is optional and self-directed keeps it in the realm of play.

And guess what, they do fewer hours than us too:

> Research studies suggest that hunter-gatherers work somewhere between 20 and 40 hours a week, on average, depending on just what you count as work. Moreover, they do not work according to the clock; they work when the time is ripe for the work to be done and when they feel like it.

> It's amazing when you think about it. During the 10,000 years since the onset of agriculture and then industry, we have developed countless labor-saving devices, but we haven't reduced our labor. Today, most people spend more time working than did hunter-gatherers, and our work, on average, is less playful.

Scrap your career plan

We must be willing to get rid of the life we've planned, so as to have the life that is waiting for us.

Joseph Campbell, mythologist, writer and lecturer

The world is changing very quickly. A five-year plan for your career or business is likely to be redundant within a few months. Jeff Bezos, CEO of trillion-dollar company Amazon, admits that "any business plan won't survive its first encounter with reality". This is even more true in the early stages of your venture – the business you start is rarely the business you end up succeeding with.

The same is true for your life as a whole. Indra Nooyi, former CEO of PepsiCo, named as one of the most powerful women in the world by both Fortune & Forbes says:

> There is nothing like a concrete life plan to weigh you down. Because if you always have one eye on some future goal, you stop paying attention to the job at hand, miss opportunities that might arise, and stay fixedly on one path, even when a better, newer course might have opened up.

The old habit of setting far-off goals and making gross compromises in the present to get there makes less and less sense. Throw your attention back on the present and embrace 'life in perpetual beta', as film-maker Melissa Pierce terms it.

Your long-term goals are not what will make you happy. Even getting rich is no guarantee. Research shows that when people win the lottery, they have a short-lived boost in happiness and then settle back to roughly the level of happiness they had before. What matters is how you choose to live today. Your aim in beginning to play is to create the positive experience you want to have in your life, starting right now even if it's scaled down to start with.

And ironically, pursuing your genuine interests, if done right, will make you richer than chasing the money ever will. You can't really excel at something when your heart isn't in it, so if you do want to get rich, choose something that feels more like play than work. It makes good business sense. You can't compete with someone who loves what they do.

My story: 'I never want another job for the rest of my life'

Many years ago when I had a job as a computer programmer, I knew I wanted something different but didn't know what it was. I realised the only way I was really going to work it out was to imagine for a moment that I could have anything I wanted.

And what I wanted was not to work.

I didn't want to sit on the sofa all day doing nothing. I wanted to play – to do whatever creative, fun stuff I love doing, and still get paid. At the time this seemed an unrealistic desire but it wasn't long after this realisation that I got exactly what I wanted. The company announced a chance for voluntary redundancies and I jumped at it. I got paid several months' salary to go and do whatever I liked. Some of my redundant colleagues bought sports cars. I didn't. I played. I created music, did some writing and I created an installation in an experimental museum. This time of play led me into the most exciting and fun job in my career. But it was still a job.

When later I had a go at stand-up comedy, I put this into my routine:

I worry I'm in the wrong job, in fact I worry I don't suit jobs. The money's OK, it's the working I have a problem with.

I think my life is just too full to fit a job in. I'm too busy doing stuff that's actually fun and that work thing just gets in the way.

My career goal is to be paid for just being me, living my life. I'm very busy, I'm putting in the hours, I should get compensated.

Name of role: being John Williams.

I'd wake up in the morning and my boss would come in and go 'Well done John, another great week, here's your wage packet.'

In reality, this is exactly what I want: to be able to do whatever I want to do, to play all day and get paid. To get paid to be me.

Not all jobs are terrible, of course. I've had some good ones – special effects software developer, online video expert, senior managing consultant for a global consultancy – but whatever the job, I still felt like life was somehow passing me by while I was stuck in front of a computer in a bland, open-plan office.

In 2003 I finally escaped and publicly declared, "I never want another job for the rest of my life." I've been working for myself ever since and conducting some interesting experiments along the way: I turned a full-time job offer into a three-day-week contract paying the same money; I earned enough as a consultant to only need to work for three months of the year; and I've enjoyed creative projects such as getting my experimental music played on radio stations around the world and sharing a part of my life story in a national newspaper.

Now I run my own business called The Ideas Lab which helps people to get clear on the work they love and turn their ideas into stand-out businesses, books and brands. Over the past 15 years we've impacted the working lives of tens of thousands of people around the world – and you can read some of their stories in this book. I've learned a lot in that time about what works in my own career and those of my clients – and what holds people back.

The work of The Ideas Lab has been featured in *The Sunday Times*, *The Times*, *The Financial Times*, *The Daily Telegraph*, *Marketing Week*, *The Daily Mail*, *Elle* magazine, *Psychologies*, *Red* and *Monocle* amongst others. And I have been interviewed on BBC Radio and on national TV in Australia.

I'm constantly fine-tuning the focus of the company and my role within it to centre on my strengths and favourite activities, whether it's writing, speaking internationally, creating innovative programmes, interviewing rule-breakers and original thinkers on The Ideas Lab podcast, or finding the creative twist in clients' ideas for businesses, books, brands and movements that makes them stand out and win instant attention. I set my own hours, choose my own co-workers and alternate my place of work between my home, my favourite café by the canal, and co-working spaces in Bali, Thailand and elsewhere.

I'm not a millionaire (yet) but my company consistently makes six figures and I've found that when I choose projects that really excite me, the company does better. My mission to get paid to play continues to evolve. It's not a project that is ever done. But it's one that I hope to convince you to start.

Let's talk about death

It might seem strange to bring death into a book about play but in fact it is at the very heart of the topic. Here's a defining event from my life that I think will show you why.

When I was five months old, my parents took me out with my brother in the family car to show me to some relatives. Just a few minutes from our home, we were hit head-on by a young drunk driver who had lost control and was on the wrong side of the road.

Both my parents were injured. My mother made a full recovery. My father died in hospital ten days later from complications with his injuries. He was 34.

Losing my father before I was even old enough to know him has coloured my whole life. It made it abundantly and painfully clear that life can end at any moment. With this stark reality in mind, now answer this question: Do you really want to spend another few years doing some unsatisfying work in the hope that you can do what you really like later?

Here's the real message of this book:

DON'T WASTE ANOTHER MINUTE OF YOUR LIFE

What do you really want your life to be about? This book will show you how to start it right now. If you don't know what you want, your mission is to find out. This book will tell you how. It's less important that you complete your work mission than that you're engaged in it. It's in the *being in play* that you will find salvation. When you are fully engaged in the right project, you will easily attract others around you who are inspired by the same aims. And if the worst happens and you don't get to complete your work yourself, others will pick up the reins.

Do what really matters. Start playing. Start now.

The first step in your journey to getting paid to play is to find out what you really want. The first Secret will show you how to discover what that is.

On the website: fworkletsplay.com

➡ Read, listen to and watch interviews with successful players, including Taylor Croonquist.

➡ Access more information and links for the people quoted.

➡ Connect with a global community of players.

Secret one

How to work out what you really really want

Too much of a good thing can be wonderful.

Mae West, American actress, playwright and screenwriter 1893–1980

The very first step to getting paid to play is to know what play feels like to you. You'll find out what that is in this Secret. And I'll show you that, no matter how impossible your ideas might seem right now, you can always have what you really really want.

If you already enjoy your work and just want to become more successful at it, you may be tempted to skip this Secret. Don't! If your work has never quite taken off, there's a good chance it's because what you're doing is not quite right yet. This Secret will help you correct your course so that you focus in on what's most enjoyable and easy for you and so get much better results for the same effort.

For the love of chocolate

Petra Barran is founder of Kerb Food, the incubator and accelerator for London's street food businesses, and she arrived at this point not through a logical career plan but purely by tuning into what she wants at each stage of her career.

My main things in life have always been love of travel and love of new people and love of food. And I've been searching my whole life for a way of turning this into something that gets me up in the morning and makes me a living – well actually, makes me a life as much as a living.

I've tried lots of different things. When I finished university I went to work for a casting director in London, looking for people for parts in TV commercials and pop videos and I used to have to go up to strangers in the street and say "Hey, you'd be great for this part." I loved it but I still had itchy feet. I just wanted to get out there and explore the world.

So I decided to run away to sea. I worked on superyachts all over the world looking after very rich people, making them cocktails, making their beds and serving them dinner. And that was fantastic but life onboard was just a little too strict and controlled for me.

While I was away I noticed that wherever I went, I was always drawn to chocolate shops. Whether I was in America, Spain, France or Israel I was always hanging out in chocolate shops looking at what everyone else was doing. And eventually I decided enough is enough. I've got to stop working on boats. I decided to go back to London with this idea that I wanted to work with chocolate and it needed to be something that allowed me to keep on moving and meeting new people. I was going to set up a chocolate business. I'm going to get a van and I'm going to turn it into a choc-mobile and I'm going to take it around the world.

Petra created Choc Star, Britain's only touring choc-mobile: a converted ice cream van that for six years travelled from market to music festival to private party to serve gourmet chocolate treats.

And then another idea came to her which would see her named as someone who changed the world of food forever. More on that in a moment.

Start from the right place

When we're trying to decide what we really want, the old-fashioned idea of work as something we have to do, rather than want to do, can all too easily get in the way. We make unnecessary compromises and limit our choices right from the start. If we become desperate to escape our current work we can end up looking for anything that seems an improvement. But that's like asking, "What's not quite as bad as this?" This is starting from the wrong place if you want to end up playing for a living. And it's a lousy question to invest your energy answering.

Here's a much better question to ask yourself: "What would work that feels like play look like for me?"

To answer it, you have to imagine you could have anything in the world. Seriously, anything. Put aside all practicalities just for a while and allow yourself to dream. If you've got stuck trying to work out what to do next, I can guarantee it's because you have failed to separate the questions "What do I want?" and "What seems possible for me right now?" Concentrate for now on the first one and we'll work out how to make it happen, or at least get as close as possible, a little later. It's essential to your success that you allow yourself to want things that you currently have no idea how you will get.

If you limit your choices only to what seems possible or reasonable, you disconnect yourself from what you truly want, and all that is left is a compromise.

Robert Fritz, composer, film-maker and organisational consultant

One of the most valuable things you can ever do is to get to know what you do and don't enjoy doing. And it can also be one of the most difficult things to do. Believe it or not, actually getting to where you want to go can seem relatively straightforward after that. It's just a list of stuff to do – call someone, write an email, turn up somewhere and do the work. If you hit an obstacle, someone will be able to tell you how to get around it.

When you know what comes most naturally to you and then centre your working life around it, leaving out as much as possible of what you don't like, you will be amazed how fast your progress can be. Your work will be like play, your passion will attract new opportunities to you every day, and your competitors will barely concern you.

Introducing your secret weapon: your playbook

Don't wait to be hit by a lightning bolt insight on what you're meant to be doing with your life. Understand instead that decisions like this are more usually built than happened upon. Build your path to playing brick by brick.

Get yourself a notebook to capture your thoughts about your transition from worker to player. Carry it everywhere. Write down everything you discover – what you like, what you don't like, people whose work or lifestyle you'd like to emulate, ideas for contacts to talk to, projects to try. This is now your *playbook*.

I'm a fan of real paper. If you are too, choose a nicely designed blank book for the purpose: one that will inspire you every time you look at it. Free yourself from the tyranny of lined paper and buy an unlined book. It allows more freedom to draw diagrams, doodles and sketches (you're not in school and no one is going to criticise your handwriting if it isn't straight). Label your playbook and add your phone number in case it gets lost (this is an important document).

Keep these notes separate from your other thoughts. Don't mix them with your diary, your creative writing or your laundry list. You need to be able to leaf through it quickly and find something that you wrote earlier.

This brings us to the first of our 21 myths that keep you stuck.

Richard Branson organises his 200-plus businesses using simple black ledger notebooks. "I can't believe when I see people not writing things down. You know they're not going to remember everything," he says. His advice is to "Always carry a little notebook in your back pocket . . . Make sure you use it for ideas, for contacts, for suggestions, for problems . . . Your life will be that much better organised for carrying it. I could never have built the Virgin Group into the size it is without those few bits of paper." He now has over a hundred black ledger notebooks that he's written in over the years.

What Columbo can teach you about discovering what you really want

I love the detective show *Columbo*. It's the ultimate wind-down TV: slow-paced and charming. The series ran for over 30 years but the classics are from the 1970s, featuring mutton chop sideburns and plots that revolve around 'cutting-edge technology' like telephone answering machines.

Lieutenant Columbo, played by the late great Peter Falk, is a homicide detective with the Los Angeles Police Department. Every feature-length episode starts by showing the actual murder scene. There is therefore no mystery, no whodunnit. The pleasure is in watching Columbo, the disheveled, apologetic cop, shambling his way towards snaring his prey and proving them guilty.

Columbo knows in the first scene who the murderer is but doesn't let on to his subject. His talent is in appearing to be harmless, enabling him to bypass the murderer's defences, while he gathers fragments of evidence that point to what really happened. Nothing goes unmissed no matter how small: a single word, a piece of lint, a sound on a recording. He jots it all down in his notebook. Columbo is troubled by details he can't resolve and he drives his suspect to distraction with his famous line 'Just one more thing. . . '

When you are on a search to discover what you'd like to do with your life, you can learn a lot from Columbo. It's time to play the detective in 'The case of the missing passion'. Your adversary is your inner critic or 'top dog' (see Secret four).

Put yourself under surveillance. No clue should go unnoticed. What part of the newspaper do you turn to first? What part of a bookshop draws you? What are your favourite TV programmes? What do you read for fun? What did you enjoy doing as a child? What kind of environment inspires you? What kind of people do you naturally get on with? What kind of daily structure suits you? What's your MO – your habits and style of working? This is all information you can use to help you on your path to play.

The evidence is there. Follow every lead and act on your hunches. This is what Petra did in her story at the start of this Secret: she acted on her hunches, played them out, and then noticed what her responses were. She knew she loved travel, food and meeting new people. When she noticed herself being drawn to chocolate shops, the last piece of the puzzle fell into place.

Carry your playbook everywhere and record every piece of evidence about what work you do like and what work you don't. Look for where the excitement is in you. Just remember that it often comes with a big dollop of fear too. We'll look at this later. If you hit a dead end, call for back-up – get help from friends or have a session with a careers or business coach.

(By the way, I think this finally shows that it's possible to turn anything that you enjoy, including lying on the sofa watching reruns on TV, into something useful for your business.)

Myth 2: The answer to my work search is in some magical new thing I have never tried before

If you're currently trapped in a job, you may be prone to thinking that there is some kind of work out there you have never tried before that is the magic solution to your dilemma. The fact is if you really love doing something, you're probably already doing it somewhere in your life. You just might not see it as something you consider work. Start the process of noting everything you enjoy and later you will see how you can get paid for it.

Stop trying to work out what to do with the rest of your life

Here's the good news: you don't need to know what you want to do with the rest of your life. In fact, asking yourself questions like that is more likely to keep you stuck. There's no way to know what the world will look like and what you'll want in ten years' time because you won't be the same person you are now. What you do in your very next step will take you in directions you could never have predicted and reveal new aspects of yourself you're not even aware of right now.

Petra Barran is a great example of this . . .

"I want something that makes me a life as much as a living"

Petra Barran had been running her gourmet choc-mobile Choc Star for some years when she had a new idea.

I took a trip to Ireland to meet friends and think over what to do next with Choc Star. As I sat in the back of a car with a

*friend driving round the skiddy January lanes in Cork, I had a
realisation – we street food traders need to start working together
in some way to really push street food forward.*

*When I got home I called my friend Giles and it turned out he'd
had a similar idea. He asked his friend Gareth to build a website
and the three of us together at my kitchen table formed the
company Eat Street.*

*We started looking out for the best street food stalls and vans
and invited them to create a profile on the website. Then we
started coordinating appearances at events. Not long after, a
developer got in touch to offer us our own site in London's Kings
Cross. We set up a market and I traded there in Choc Star with
up to five other Eat Street members at a time.*

*Then when my own van Choc star was six years old, I realised
I was ready to hang up my ice cream scoops. I sold the van to
concentrate on Eat Street.*

Eat Street went on to play a key role in what became a London
street food revolution, resulting in Petra being selected as one of
The Independent's 'Ten People who Changed the World'. But she
wanted to go further . . .

*After a year of Eat Street I thought this could be a real business,
but my two co-founders didn't have the same vision of where to
take it. I realised I'd have to break away and we went through a
very painful 'divorce' period.*

*In the end we dissolved Eat Street and I founded Kerb Food, an
organisation that helps people launch their street food business
and have a better shot at success.*

*We run workshops for those with an idea for a street food van, we
spot talent and help incubate businesses, we accelerate existing
ones and connect businesses with investors. And meanwhile*

we are raising both the visibility and the quality bar so that street food is always moving forward.

In 2019 KERB street food markets sold over 10,000 dishes a week at five markets across London. Several popular KERB businesses have gone on to become restaurants. KERB also opened a permanent market in London's Convent Garden which hosts 25 vendors including the world's first cheese conveyor belt restaurant.

Read more about Kerb at www.kerbfood.com

If trying to see into your distant future is stressing you out, let's think a little more in the short term. Here's an exercise that will help you get a lot closer to discovering what you really want to do.

Let's take a year out

How would you like to take a year off? Let's say the whole of the next 12 months. Sounds appealing? OK, I hereby give you my permission. Done.

Yes, I know you have a few practical concerns such as what you'll live on but let's dream a little. Imagine I'd just handed you a year's salary so you don't need to earn anything. Think about this for a moment – next Friday is now your last day in your current work. Now, what is it you're going to do in this precious year of total freedom? Spend a year sitting on the beach, doing nothing? Or do you know that after the first few weeks, you'd be itching to do something else? If so, what? What exactly *will* you do for the other 11 months?

Maybe you'll do some projects you've been wanting to do for a long time: write a book, start your own business, go study something you're fascinated by, travel the world, do up your home, get serious about your photography, hold your own exhibition, dive into futurology, attend conferences and share what you learn on

YouTube, become a public speaker, get into TV, go work alongside a hero of yours, or change some piece of the world for the better.

Or perhaps now you're free of work, you'll take the time to address some part of your personal life: cure that rumbling medical gripe, work out how to make yourself genuinely happy, create a fulfilling relationship, or heal a rift in your family?

Whatever it might be, at 5pm next Friday you are free at last. What will you do?

Among my clients, Philip would build a kick-arse inventor workshop, Sally would fiddle with things, make things, and spend time inspiring people; Neil would be studying integral philosophy, Juliette would sail across the Atlantic and share her journey online, and Emma would be living by the sea, with a pet dog and indulging her love of photography.

Write it down. Turn to a blank page in your playbook (or grab the nearest scrap of paper – don't get precious about this) and write down all the things you would like to do in your year of play. If anything requires more money than is available in your annual salary, I am granting you a limitless fund for any experience you want to have. This is not about buying new shiny things, it's so that there is nothing in the way of having the experiences you want – round-the-world air ticket or the money to buy that castle you want to renovate – it's all possible now.

Of course, when you begin your year of total freedom you might just want to take a long holiday or catch up with friends. Make a note of this, but then start to think of what you might do after a couple of months of chill-out and catch-up.

Need a little more inspiration?

Still sketchy about what projects you'd take on in your year of play? Here are five questions to consider that will help spark your creative engine.

Looking back over your career, when were you most happy?

Write down any moments that occur to you. It may have been something that was not a central part of your work but you really enjoyed anyway: organising the Christmas party, competing in the office football league. Write it down, then think about what it was that made this so enjoyable for you. You might choose to include some element of this in your year out.

Who is your career hero?

Is there someone whose life or work you really admire? Who is it? It could be someone famous, someone from history, someone you know or even someone fictional. What is it about them you most admire? Is it the field they work in, the results they create or the attitude they have that you're impressed by? What project or achievement of theirs stands out for you? Write it all down in your playbook. If several people come to mind, write them all down.

One of my career heroes is musician, producer, visual artist and creative thinker Brian Eno. He once wrote a diary for a year and published it as a book. He wrote in the introduction, "I have a wonderful life. I do pretty much what I want, and the only real problem I ever have is wondering what that is." His career is enormously varied. He is very successful and hugely respected in his field, yet almost unheard of by the majority of the population and so is free to walk down the street unnoticed. This sounds like the ideal working life to me. What's yours? What elements of their lives would you want to re-create in your year of freedom?

Who do you envy?

Whose working life are you envious of? What aspect of this person's work makes you most envious? When I am helping clients with their careers or businesses I very occasionally get envious of them. The two times that stand out for me were with people moving into working for large cutting-edge creative agencies. These are high-profile organisations that are tough to get into. One client resorted to baking a cake for the company and writing his CV in icing on the top just to get an interview. (It worked.)

Envy is a useful thing. It tells me there's something I still don't have. In this case, I worked out that I needed to bring more of my love of design into my work. I've done this by working with great designers to help create the brand of several businesses, and setting up my office in a loft-style live/work space.

Sometimes envy will reveal something you can't access any other way. Ask people what's their ideal work and a lot of people are stumped. Ask whose job, business or lifestyle they most envy and you get some useful information. As long as you don't stay with the envy and imagine you're powerless to have the thing you want, you can use it.

Envy implies that you want something that is out of reach to you. Recognising the envy is useful if you can remove the block to getting it. To do this, imagine hiring the very person you envy to train you step by step to get the thing you want. What advice do you think they would give you? What would they need to teach you? Perhaps you'd need to borrow some of their resources and contacts too. With all this at your disposal, what project would you now take on? Write it down.

What do you find difficult to stop doing?

What do you hate not to be doing? What do you find yourself squeezing into stolen moments? What is difficult for you to stop doing when you should be getting on with your work? Write it all down. Which of these would you do more of in your year out?

What projects would you take on if you knew you couldn't fail?

Write a novel? Become a rock star? Climb the Matterhorn? Find a cure for cancer? Overthrow the government? Write down your answer. Add some version of it into your year off. No matter how grand your dream, there will be a way to have a taste of it.

Too many things to do to fit into one year?

By this point, you may be looking at your notes and feeling alarmed at the number of things you want to do.

Myth 3: I should be able to find one thing that interests me and stick to it

The traditional world of work tries to cram everything that we are into a narrow box and give it a single label: programmer, accountant, designer, writer. We are all far more than one label can contain: we are 'slashes': programmer/social activist, accountant/business coach, interior designer/TV personality/musician, writer/public speaker/parent . . . and more.

When you design a working life from scratch, there is no need to hide away any part of you anymore. As a player, you can bring all of who you are to your work and be all the more valuable as a result.

Your interests will naturally change, evolve and expand over time. As they do, you can reposition your work to suit. It's possible that what you're currently doing was once exciting and challenging but now feels dull. That's natural. The most exciting projects and tasks are always at the edge of our abilities. Once we've mastered them, they lose their shine and we're ready for the next thing.

We each have a different pace at which we like to evolve our work. What's yours? Are you happy to go deep into a topic and specialise for several years before you move on? Or do you get bored easily and have to keep switching to something new to keep your interest? If you're in the latter group who likes to chop and change frequently, you're what American careers guru Barbara Sher calls a 'scanner'.

ARE YOU A SCANNER?

This is the age of the scanner and the polymath – fast learners with multiple interests and multiple strings to their bows who can curate and synthesise diverse topics and disciplines into something entirely new.

So are you a scanner?

Try asking yourself the following questions:

1. Are you interested in lots of different, and seemingly unrelated things?

2. Are you fascinated by something different every week?

3. Does the thought of concentrating on one topic, skill or job for very long horrify you?

4. Do you start lots of projects but move on before you finish them?

If you answered yes to more than one of these then you are almost certainly a scanner. A scanner is someone who loves to learn and explore new things but gets bored quickly. Scanners are about breadth rather than depth. We want to learn just enough about something to understand the most interesting bits of it and then move on to the next thing.

Scanners are also sometimes referred to as Renaissance men or women, just like the most famous scanner of all, Leonardo da Vinci. Leonardo was a scientist, mathematician, engineer, inventor, anatomist, painter, sculptor, architect, botanist, musician and writer. And he often didn't finish the projects he started. So if that sounds like you, you're in good company.

Entrepreneurs are often scanners and polymaths, using their enthusiasm for starting things and love of learning to good effect. The five largest companies in the world today were all founded by polymaths: Bill Gates, Steve Jobs, Warren Buffett, Larry Page and Jeff Bezos. Even if your aims are more modest, multiple academic studies have found a correlation between the number of interests and competencies someone has and their creative impact.

I am a scanner and my breadth of interests, unending curiosity and ability to learn quickly are a huge help in being able to assist a wide range of people launch and market businesses in anything from online training courses to therapy to software start-ups.

From school teacher to ukulele entrepreneur with multiple side-projects

Sarah Weiler was teaching Spanish and German in a secondary school in Uxbridge when she first read my book. She wrote comedy songs about her students in her spare time and dreamed of escaping teaching:

> Being a teacher taught me so many great skills but it was exhausting to be 'on' all day in front of a class. I wanted to do something where I could spend more time reflecting, creating and planning.

> One rainy January following Latin beats at a Zumba class, my housemate and I decided to quit in the summer term and go to South America. We travelled through South America for a few months and then I got a job at a teaching organisation in Argentina. I had the best international house-share in Buenos Aires, and it was there I first learned the ukulele.

Next, I landed a job in a teaching organisation in Vienna. I learned a lot there but the climate was tough, so I wrote a song on the ukulele and suggested that all the staff sing it. Although that initially met with resistance, the uke and singing together became a huge lifeline for our company culture that first year, and without knowing it my future business was forming.

I travelled next to Columbia for another education project and while I was there, my staff at Teach for Austria had sent me a video of them all playing the ukulele together at a staff meeting. An image came to me at that moment of doing corporate ukulele workshops. I started running uke meet-ups in Brixton to practise teaching it to groups.

Then Sarah took a course with me to launch a creative project in 30 days.

I wrote '30 minutes of comedy in 30 days' and then realising it would be difficult to get someone to give me a 30-minute slot at an established comedy night, I decided to put on my own comedy show with other comedians and performers.

We sold out a top room of a pub in Peckham in London and the landlord asked us if we wanted to run it regularly. My friend Rose was at the bar with me and she said she'd run it with me, and Rye Laughs was born.

A few months later, a friend and I met on a Sunday to play music and do creative things. An excited conversation ended up with us posting on Facebook: "Who wants to come to the countryside and be creative for the weekend?" We found a venue and filled all the places in 48 hours. This was the first of four Creative Retreats over two years, helping people reconnect with their creativity in the beautiful countryside.

Not long after I bought 30 ukuleles and I got my first booking for 'Power of Uke.' That year was spent building up a website and trialling workshops. And in 2016 Power of Uke got its first big corporate gig.

Selling ukulele workshops to large corporations might seem unlikely but Sarah explains:

This is much more than a music workshop. I use learning to play the ukulele from scratch as a metaphor for taking on a challenge that seems impossible. I describe it as teaching 21st century skills – empathy, creativity, growth mindset and dealing with uncertainty.

As we go through the class, I often stop and ask people what is going on for them. When I get a room full of lawyers to the point where they're willing to admit they don't know what they're doing and they're OK with that, everyone feels relieved.

In 2017 AirBnB approached me to be one of its pilot 'experiences' featured on the front page of its website, running ukulele walking tours. I took London visitors on a tour of the city and taught them songs as we walked around the capital's landmarks.

Then I landed a huge contract with one of the big four accounting firms which really boosted my confidence and took my business to the next level. Today, I am regularly running Power of Uke for Google Sprint Labs and I've also worked with Microsoft, HelloFresh, AIB bank and others and been featured in The Daily Telegraph.

Sarah says the key is making variety work as an entrepreneur:

I still want to keep the variety of my other scanner projects. The Rye Laughs comedy night just celebrated its fifth birthday and is going strong. And I still have time for other projects as they occur to me – I recently won a DJing spot at Glastonbury Festival and I gave a TEDx talk called 'Knowing When to Quit'. I've realised that there is a common theme in most of the things I do – space-holding, creating an atmosphere for people to thrive but also to have fun and play.

When I first read your book, I did an exercise to design my ideal day in a notebook. I wrote that I would be getting up late, going to a coffee shop, chatting to people, delivering a workshop, and performing stand-up. And that's now my life!

I ended the past decade feeling really proud of how I've grown, noticing that most of the things in my life are things that bring me joy and that I would choose to do, whether I was being paid or not. Looking ahead at the coming year there is a lot of space, and part of me feels anxious to fill it, but I also am really excited to see what ideas and projects appear over the next few years, as long as I keep following the joy. . .

Read more about Sarah and The Power of Uke at *powerofuke.com*

Whether you're a scanner or you like to dive deep into a topic for longer, the important thing is to craft a life that suits you. (If you like to specialise, your year off might be about throwing yourself into a year of intense study.)

POWER-UP: The scanner's guide to success

I have met hundreds, if not thousands, of scanners over the last 15 years. For five years I ran a popular live event in London called Scanners Night with guest speakers on topics of creativity, fast learning and productivity for people with multiple interests. I've also helped many scanners start a business they would never get bored of.

In all those years I have seen some scanners create remarkable, original and successful businesses that keep them endlessly engaged while others seem to never progress, dabbling with multiple projects and never moving forward. I've noticed what makes the difference. So if you want to be in the first group, use these seven guidelines to scanner success.

▶

1. **Choose a project or business that will retain your interest** Choose something multifaceted with variety and lots of new things to learn. Find a way to use your skill to come up with new ideas or do research without having to do all the implementation yourself.

   Scanners make great journalists, comedians, cultural commentators, consultants, public speakers, researchers, inventors and entrepreneurs – anything that maximises the ability to learn quickly, make creative connections, communicate what you found, and move on. Many of these also allow you to work on a range of projects with a wide variety of people and organisations so that you don't get bored.

   Try to find other people to do the follow-through work we scanners are bad at, such as detailed editing, project planning or financial management.

2. **Look for the theme in your passions** Look for the common theme in the things you love, because while it might present itself in different ways over the years you will never bore of the theme.

   For Sarah Weiler it was creating a space for people to thrive while also having fun – whether that's a comedy club, learning ukulele in a corporate workshop, or a creative retreat.

   For me, it is a love of the new – I am drawn to new and surprising ways of doing familiar things. You'll read examples throughout this book from an innovative stop smoking app to healthy ice cream to silent dating events. And I have built my business around my favourite activity: helping people to create a unique business or product of their own. For me this is getting paid to play and I will never tire of it.

3. **Consider creating a business that combines your interests** Some of the happiest scanners have combined

several of their interests into their own business. I have done this myself with my company The Ideas Lab. I've managed to combine many of my strongest interests from creativity, psychology, writing, online marketing, technology, design, and online user experience into a whole.

And when you combine several skills you have into your career choice you often find you have created a competitive advantage that is hard to beat.

In addition, when you run your own business you are actually forced (at least initially) to take on a wide range of activities since there is no one else in your team. This is a welcome change for scanners who found themselves stuck in a silo in their corporate life.

There is no limit to how successful scanners can be. Some of our most famous entrepreneurs are examples: from Richard Branson to Oprah Winfrey to Elon Musk.

4. **Know your cash cow** If you are going to have a lot of loosely related projects and ventures, you will most likely find that one of them is your main earner, your *cash cow*. Be clear about what will be your cash cow (for Sarah it's the Power of Uke) and don't get so distracted that you let it lapse.

Once you know your cash cow and you can earn enough from it while not taking up all your time, you are free to do any project you like in the rest of your time, whether it makes a lot of money, a little extra income, or no money at all.

Remember that not all of your projects need to make money. It's perfectly OK to label some as pure fun or a hobby.

Sometimes however, you might find you can turn one of more of your wackier ideas into something that, while it doesn't make much money directly, it helps promote your personal brand or business. Sarah Weiler, for instance, occasionally

▶

runs fun, affordable ukulele events for the general public that draw attention to the work she does for corporations.

5. **Become T-shaped** Our breadth of knowledge can be valuable in itself but it is even more so when you combine it with a depth of expertise in a particular skill or topic. This has been termed a 'T-shaped personality'. While many people are I-shaped with deep expertise in just one narrow topic, scanners have the potential to become T-shaped. Their breadth of knowledge allows them to connect with other disciplines but combine it with an expertise in a particular area that allows them to create something very valuable.

   If you love learning a new topic every month for instance, this in itself won't get you paid. Combine it with getting really good at a valuable skill such as teaching, writing or speaking. If you have a love of new ideas for products and businesses, bear in mind you can't get paid for ideas alone. But develop an expertise in digital marketing, branding or design and you can get paid to add your creative magic to a variety of new businesses.

6. **Follow through on the things that matter** As scanners we are great at starting things and not so good at finishing them. That's OK when it's a fun dive into a new language to understand the basics but if you want to have a satisfying work–life you need to follow through on your more important projects to the point where you produce something you can share with others. More on this in Secret 3.

7. **Only launch one project at a time** If you are trying to get a new career or business off the ground, only launch one at a time. Projects require the most energy and attention when they are first launched. Get something working to a point where it doesn't need your constant attention before thinking of launching another project.

> If you are reading this book to find something to replace your current income, your first project should to be to create your cash cow. Once you've got that working you can explore other ideas.

Let's return to our 'year off' exercise. Whether you're a scanner or not, if the thought of choosing only one year off is stressing you out, here's an exercise that will help.

Welcome to the universe(s)

I have an uncle who is an astrophysicist and works at large observatories around the world. I was on the phone to him one Christmas and trying to think of something to talk about with this very intelligent but rather introverted man. Running out of small talk, I asked, "So what's new in physics?" After a considerable silent pause while he gathered his thoughts, he said in his slow, doleful, voice, "Well, there's a lot of interest at the moment in wormholes between parallel universes." "Wait a minute, back up a bit," I said, "Are you telling me there are parallel universes?' "Well yes, that's the best thinking at the current time," he calmly replied. Somehow this rather incredible information had not ended up on the front page of the newspapers.

Some experts in quantum physics go as far as to suggest that every time a decision is made, the universe splits into two – one where the first choice plays out and another where the opposite choice plays out. We don't yet know how to move between these worlds, but until my uncle cracks it, it's a very useful idea to consider. Because now you don't just have one year off, you have infinite variations of your year off.

Let's just take the first seven of them. Realising you can live seven completely different years off, write down what you will do in each one. In universe one you might become an entrepreneur and get rich; in universe two perhaps you train in medicine and research new treatments; in universe three you could become a full-time parent; in universe four you become a social activist; in universe five a famous comedian – and you still have two left. Write them all down in your playbook.

But isn't all this totally unrealistic?

A little bit. But you can have what you want a lot more often than you think. If you don't at least know what you want, what chance do you have of getting it?

Aside from this, knowing yourself, what you like and what you want out of life is a fundamental skill in creating a life you love – and it's one you can practise. Until you are in tune with who you are, you will struggle to make the right decisions and create a career you enjoy.

And while some of your ideas won't ever be part of your paid work, you would be surprised how often it *is* possible to turn a passion into something that gets you paid directly – or at least plays a part in your business and personal brand.

Here's the good news: you can have what you *really* want

Here's the thing: no matter how crazy your dream is of getting paid to play, you can always have the part you really want. Even if you can't have the exact vision you see in your mind, you will be able to have the part that's most exciting to you as long as you're flexible about how you get it.

Here's the critical question most people never ask themselves: What is the *experience* you want to have in this vision of your ideal work? Plenty of people might have the same dream – for instance, to be a rock star – but the reasons will differ. What's the part you really want? What's the experience of being a rock star that matters to you? For some it's performing in front of an audience and being the centre of attention, while for others it's being rich or being creative, or it's the status of being known and respected. Or it's being a rebel, or touring the country with a group, or controlling your own life. (And for some I guess it's the sex and drugs but we'll leave that to one side for now.)

Once you know what the experience is that you really want, you can be sure you will get it when you go for the dream. And even more importantly, if you decide not to go for your original dream, there are then many ways you can have the part you want most.

Imagine a lawyer who dreams of being a rock star. He realises he loves the reliable salary of a job so decides not to risk it all for rock stardom. Instead, he gets a job in the legal department of a record company because that seems a good alternative. The problem is that the experience of his job is largely the same and what he does day to day hasn't changed. He still sits in an office and writes contracts all day but now every so often Katy Perry walks past his desk. If the experience he wants is to perform in front of an audience, he might find that getting a slot on TV as a legal expert or giving talks at major conferences is far more satisfying.

Back to you. Write down in your playbook the experience you want to have when you think of your dream work. What's the essence of your ideal vision that's most important to you? What's the most exciting part? Be completely honest with yourself and don't worry what anyone else might think. If you want to be world famous, or you want to get rich, or you realise that the most exciting thing in the world to you is to pore over 30 pages of financial figures, don't let anyone else's opinion of what's selfish or superficial or weird or boring get in the way. Just write it down.

Myth 4: I can't do what I want to do without long expensive training

A common stumbling block is that what you want to do requires long and expensive training. If you don't want to do this or can't afford it, with some creativity you can usually think of a different way to get the experience you want to have. Get clear what the part is that you're most drawn to and find a different way to get that without the long training.

We get stuck when we think it's the dream or nothing. In fact, the dream is just a signpost to an experience you want more of. It's an indicator of what you need for the next stage of your own development. And this development is a natural part of being human that continues throughout our lives if we don't block it. You might find at one point in your life that you feel drawn to leading a team, or climbing to the top of the corporate ladder. And once you've had that experience, you might then be drawn to go and work for yourself. Each experience builds on the last and it's impossible to tell in advance where the next one will lead you. If you ignore whatever is your current itch, you won't get to find out just what interesting places it might take you.

Some of what you've written in these exercises might surprise you, though it might seem kind of random right now. Just trust that if you can find a way to have the experience you want next, you will keep moving towards work that is more satisfying – and you'll keep developing as a person. All living organisms have this same drive towards growth and self-expression: a tree will keep growing to its full genetic potential as long as it has the space and the sustenance it needs.

Musicians must make music, artists must paint, poets must write if they are to be ultimately at peace with themselves. What human beings can be, they must be.

Abraham Maslow, American psychologist, 1908–70

When you are truly in play, when you are following the unfolding path of what provides you with engagement, expression, excitement and curiosity in the world, then your work is simply a natural expression of who you are and who you are becoming. This is the revolutionary shift from living as a worker to living as a player.

Work becomes a way of achieving the fullest expression of yourself. At its deepest level, it's a channel, as author David Deida says, for giving your love to the world.

So if you ask, "Can I really have what I want in my work?", the answer is of course you can, because everyone can move towards their fullest expression of themselves. Everyone can decide to give their love to the world in their work. The only person blocking you from doing that is you. Open your mind and you'll see there's always a way to have the experience you are craving in your work. And you'll see later how you can guarantee you get it.

Introducing Play Wednesday

Here's an exercise that will help you envision your life of play in detail and let you have a taste of it right now.

Let's zoom in on your year of play. Fast-forward three months and imagine you're well into your year of freedom. You've got the life you've always wanted and you're having a ball. It's Wednesday, and a particularly excellent Wednesday at that. What does it look like? Where are you living? What time do you get up? What do you do first? What time do you start your activities for the day? Where do you go to do them? What are you doing? Who with? What happens the rest of the day? What time do you finish? What do you do afterwards? Write it all down in your playbook.

Of course, you probably can't take the whole year off work in reality, but you can begin to build some of that ideal experience into your life right now. Wednesday is a great day to experiment with this. Halfway between weekends, it's the ideal time to build a little play into your work week – turn hump day into a play day.

As I write here, it is in fact Wednesday. I'm sitting in a co-working space on Koh Lanta island in Thailand looking out on to the tropical garden and surrounded by friendly digital nomads from all over the world. Today I am focusing on writing all day and interviewing people over Skype who have used the ideas in this book to create remarkable working lives and businesses. I took time to have a swim before work and later, a group of us will have dinner at one of the many restaurants by the beach. This is not some unattainable millionaire lifestyle. It is something possible for many of us to create if we dare to choose it. See Secret 10 for more on becoming a digital nomad.

Make Wednesday every week a day when you get a little bit closer to your ideal life. Take some time first thing in the morning, or in the afternoon if you have the option, or in the evening after work. Note it in your diary to remind yourself every week. Even if you can only grab a few minutes out of your day, do it.

If you want to be a poet, take a book of poems to read and a notebook to write in on your commute. If you're excited about share dealing, make a little time to read the financial news or a book on the stock market. Then find ways to free up more time as the weeks go on so you can get closer to your ideal. Why not really throw yourself into it and take the day off to try living as you would like? If your dream is to live by the sea, take a trip to the coast and spend a day living like a local. Exercises where individuals design their ideal day (as Sarah Weiler did), and then set about creating it, have been scientifically proven to add to your happiness, so it's well worth doing.

In the next Secret you'll find out how to choose what to do next to bring you a step closer to making your vision of a year out a reality.

Put it into play

Keys to this secret:

➡ Start thinking with a blank slate about what you really really want. Imagine your year of play and write it down – where, who what.

➡ Don't wait for inspiration. Build your decision: write down everything you discover about what you do and don't want in your work. Start by listing five things you do want and five things you don't want.

➡ Get clear what the experience is that you really want to have. There is always a way to have this.

What you should have now:

➡ A vision of your ideal working life.

➡ Some idea of the experience you want to have from the next stage of your working life.

Take ten minutes to play:

➡ Look online for a playbook you like and order it.

➡ Write Play Wednesday in your diary as a repeating appointment to live a little of your year out.

➡ Live a little of your year of play right now. Give yourself a small taste today of what your year of play would be about. You may need to apply some seriously lateral thinking to do so. If you would like to be living in Japan but right now it seems impossible, get yourself a novel to read that's set in the country, watch films and documentaries about the place, eat the food, listen to Japanese music, book yourself a language course, or go to a language exchange evening.

It's not meant to be a substitute for the real thing, but it will give you a taste. It will engage your creativity and, hopefully leave you in a happy and positive state of mind – which is the best possible state in which to make real changes to your life. In the next Secret, we'll look at how to get you a little closer to the real year-off experience.

Exclusive extras on fworkletsplay.com:

➡ More advice for Scanners.

➡ Interviews with people featured in this Secret.

➡ Information on how to get personal help working out what you really want to do.

Secret two
How to choose what to do next

Where the needs of the world and your talents cross, there lies your vocation.

Aristotle 348–322BC

You should now have some ideas for what you would do with your time if you had complete freedom. You've looked at the things you enjoy doing and the experiences you want to have. But how does all this translate into a possible direction for your work? And how do you know which thread to pursue? This secret will help you pick a direction to investigate further. Here's a great story about just such a career decision.

Paul McCartney, coil winder

In 1961 Paul McCartney had a choice to make: to keep his safe job as a coil winder in a Liverpool factory or to pursue his dreams with the Beatles. He explains what happened next:

> I started working at a coil-winding factory called Massey and Coggins. My dad had told me to go out and get a job. I'd said, "I've got a job, I'm in a band." But after a couple of weeks of doing nothing with the band it was, "No, you have got to get a proper job." He virtually chucked me out of the house. So I went to the employment office and said, "Can I have a job? Just give me anything." And the first job was sweeping the yard at Massey and Coggins. I took it.
>
> I went there and the personnel officer said, "We can't have you sweeping the yard, you're management material." And they

started to train me from the shop floor up with that in mind. Of course, I wasn't very good on the shop floor – I wasn't a very good coil-winder.

One day John and George showed up in the yard that I should have been sweeping and told me we had a gig at the Cavern. I said, "No. I've got a steady job here and it pays £7 14s a week. They are training me here. That's pretty good, I can't expect more." And I was quite serious about this.

But then . . . I thought, "Sod it. I can't stick this lot." I bunked over the wall and was never seen again by Massey and Coggins. Pretty shrewd move really, as things turned out.

Paul McCartney from *The Beatles Anthology*

It takes bravery to dare to do what you really want to do. And you may need to challenge some of the popular myths about work, like the following old classic.

Myth 5: Doing what you love is selfish

One of the most destructive myths in life is that doing what you love to do and steering away from the things you don't is being selfish. But remember that we enjoy doing the things that we are good at. And we are drawn to the things that are most important to the next stage of our development as human beings.

When you hold back from using your unique mix of talents, you actually short-change your company, your clients and even the human race. *That* is being selfish. And everybody loses – you impoverish the world. What would have happened if Paul McCartney had stayed working as a rather unmotivated coil-winder and written off his part in the Beatles as self-indulgent nonsense?

Who knows if you'll reach the dizzying heights that Paul did? It doesn't matter. Better for everyone that you do what you're really good at and love to do than be yet another example of mediocrity.

Remember it's not all about you. If you're a blocked artist, or you've written something but never shown it to anyone, or you've got an idea to improve your industry but you think you're not qualified to make suggestions, it's easy to get wound up in your own internal battle. But it's not just about you. Everyone misses out when you hold back. Maybe your first bit of writing won't be fantastic, but it will lay the foundations for your next piece. And if nothing else, when you dare to do something you care about, you inspire others to do what they care about.

Staying in ill-fitting work is detrimental to your happiness. Your self-esteem is dependent on feeling capable and if all the feedback about your work is negative, you won't feel that. It's important to start making your shift into something better suited as soon as you can.

How do you know what to invest your time in playing? Well first, playing at whatever you feel drawn to regardless of potential income – pure play – is a valuable pursuit in itself, at least for a while. Why? Because it's fun (and fun is good for you) and it gets you into motion. It helps you discover what you like (and what you don't), what you're good at (and what you're not so good at), and it develops new skills and emerging aspects of your personality that can grow into a whole new direction for your life. If you've been stuck for a long time on what to do next in your work, and you can afford some time for experimentation, it's worth choosing almost anything you're really keen to do and having a play with it for a few weeks.

But how do you ensure you can eventually get paid and you don't just play your way to poverty? The key is that some of your play must meet a need that people have. Besides, the latest psychological research shows that the happiest people in the world use their natural strengths in the service of others.

The happiness equation

Want to know the magic formula for a happy and fulfilling life? Here it is:

Pleasure + Engagement + Meaning = Happiness

Pleasure is experiencing positive emotions from enjoying activities and relationships: a great meal, riding your bike, a picnic in the park with someone you love. And it's also the ability to notice and savour these experiences as they happen. Just recalling a positive experience that happened to you yesterday has been shown to make you measurably happier.

Engagement is the experience of getting lost in something you find so satisfying that you lose track of time and hours fly by in moments. It's being in play, absorbed in those activities you imagined in your year out.

Meaning is about using your strengths in the service of a cause greater than yourself, making a contribution to something beyond the boundaries of your own life.

To be both happy and satisfied with your life, you need all three of these elements. We often mistakenly believe pleasure is all you need to be happy but in fact the good feelings from pleasurable experiences tend not to last very long. When the experience is over, the good feelings quickly subside. However, being in service, doing something good for others brings good feelings that persist after the event is over.

When you're immersed in something that feels like play, you are likely to experience both pleasure and engagement. The third element is to use your play to help others. If you want to get paid to play, connecting with the needs of others will ensure you don't play your way to poverty.

Here's the thing. As soon as we start talking about helping others, a whole lot of 'shoulds' appear and we start imagining that we must volunteer to make tea at the old people's home or go live in some poverty-stricken part of the world. We fall into the do-gooder trap. If you feel passionate about doing those things, go do them. Otherwise, find another way to support the same cause using your strengths. We're trying to find something that suits *you*, remember? What I'm talking about here is doing what you genuinely enjoy *and* finding a way to help others while doing it. Read on for a simple exercise that will help you find a way to do this. It might just change the entire focus of your work.

Find your moment

There are already moments in your life when you use your natural strengths to help others. Think back to a recent time in your work that stands out as a great moment: one when you did something you know you are great at, you really enjoyed doing it, and it had a positive impact. What were you doing at that moment? What made it so enjoyable for you?

Your moment may come in many different forms: coming up with the new idea that makes a whole project run better; making a great joke in the middle of a presentation; saying something encouraging to a co-worker when they most need it; negotiating a huge discount on a purchase; pointing someone to just the right piece of information; tweaking a process or system to make it better; finding a clever way to automate a task; spotting the error in a plan before it starts. Look for something you got a great deal of pleasure out of – not just for the result (like a pat on the back from your boss or client) – but in the actual doing of it.

This moment may not be something that is in your job description or is one of your main business tasks – setting up your computer for maximum productivity or writing a funny email for a colleague's birthday. If your current work is so off the mark that you can't think of a single moment of this kind, look at your personal life for moments when you do something brilliantly, enjoy it and it's valuable to other people. Often this thing took you very little time at all to do – even if a huge amount of experience and preparation led up to it.

This is your *moment of magic*. Write it down in your playbook. Think of two or three other moments that stand out and write these down too. Can you see any common element that makes them so special to you? Write it down if so, but don't worry if not.

Now here's a thought. How often are you doing your moment of magic currently in your work? Once a day? Once a week? Once a month? Only in your spare time? Imagine if you just did your moment of magic twice as often in a week. How much more valuable would you be to your employer or your business? You might find you were twice as valuable. Now imagine expanding this moment so that your whole career revolves around it and your working week centres on having these moments. How much fun would that be? How valuable would you be? Can you see that it might be possible for you to get paid for all that value?

How to get into flow

Your moment of magic is you at your best. It's an experience of being in flow. This means doing those things that you are naturally talented at and enjoy doing. To get paid to play, you must spend as much time as possible in flow. Personality profiling is excellent to help you do this. If we all knew ourselves thoroughly and were totally in touch with what we liked and didn't like, we wouldn't need personality-profiling systems. We would know exactly what work we should each be doing and we would happily appreciate other people's different ways of thinking and acting. Meanwhile, in the real world, we can benefit from something that shows us our best traits and the patterns of the work that does and doesn't suit us.

There are many personality profiling systems but for our purposes the most important thing to get from such a system is an understanding of your strengths and weaknesses so that you know what you should major on and what you should find others to do.

The Belbin team roles are great at this. They were originally developed by Dr Meredith Belbin as part of a unique study of teams that took place at Henley Business School in the UK. The Belbin roles do not tell you what job you should do or what business you should run. Instead, they show you the part you should play in any project or business. This is your 'path of least resistance'. When you stick to it, work feels like play and you achieve success, wealth and impact quicker and with far less effort.

There are nine profiles. Read the descriptions below and see which ones resonate with you most. There are likely to be two or three. To know for sure, you can take an online test for which there is a small fee (£42 at the time of writing but for a limited time you can save 10% by entering the code IDP10j2x). However, even without taking the test, I hope this will make it clear how valuable it is to know your personality type and its strengths and weaknesses. Although these are described as team roles, if you are starting your own business you might be the only team member but this will show what you need to outsource to someone else first.

Which profile are you?

Belbin team roles

Plant
Tends to be highly creative and good at solving problems in unconventional ways.

Strengths: Creative, imaginative, free-thinking, generates ideas and solves difficult problems.

Allowable weaknesses: Might ignore incidentals, may be too preoccupied to communicate effectively.

Don't be surprised to find that: They could be absent-minded or forgetful.

Monitor evaluator
Provides a logical eye, making impartial judgements where required and weighs up the company or team's options in a dispassionate way.

Strengths: Sober, strategic and discerning. Sees all options and judges accurately.

Allowable weaknesses: Sometimes lacks the drive and ability to inspire others and can be overly critical.

Don't be surprised to find that: They could be slow to come to decisions.

Co-ordinator
Needed to focus on the team or organisation's objectives, draw out team members and delegate work appropriately.

Strengths: Mature, confident. Identifies talent and clarifies goals.

Allowable weaknesses: Can be seen as manipulative and might offload their own share of the work.

Don't be surprised to find that: They might over-delegate, leaving themselves little work to do.

Resource investigator
Uses their inquisitive nature to find ideas to bring back to the organisation.

Strengths: Outgoing, enthusiastic. Explores opportunities and develops contacts.

▶

Allowable weaknesses: Might be over-optimistic, and can lose interest once the initial enthusiasm has passed.

Don't be surprised to find that: They might forget to follow up on a lead.

Implementer

Needed to plan a workable strategy and carry it out as efficiently as possible.

Strengths: Practical, reliable, efficient. Turns ideas into actions and organises work that needs to be done.

Allowable weaknesses: Can be a bit inflexible and slow to respond to new possibilities.

Don't be surprised to find that: They might be slow to relinquish their plans in favour of positive changes.

Completer finisher

Most effectively used at the end of tasks to polish and scrutinise the work for errors, subjecting it to the highest standards of quality control.

Strengths: Painstaking, conscientious, anxious. Searches out errors. Polishes and perfects.

Allowable weaknesses: Can be inclined to worry unduly, and reluctant to delegate.

Don't be surprised to find that: They could be accused of taking their perfectionism to extremes.

Teamworker

Helps get people to gel, using their versatility to identify the work required and complete it on behalf of the team or organisation.

Strengths: Co-operative, perceptive and diplomatic. Listens and averts friction.

Allowable weaknesses: Can be indecisive in crunch situations and tends to avoid confrontation.

Don't be surprised to find that: They might be hesitant to make unpopular decisions.

Shaper

Provides the necessary drive to ensure that the organisation or team keeps moving and does not lose focus or momentum.

Strengths: Challenging, dynamic. Thrives on pressure. Has the drive and courage to overcome obstacles.

Allowable weaknesses: Can be prone to provocation, and may sometimes offend people's feelings.

Don't be surprised to find that: They could risk becoming aggressive and bad-humoured in their attempts to get things done.

Specialist

Brings in-depth knowledge of a key area to the organisation or project.

Strengths: Single-minded, self-starting and dedicated. Provides specialist knowledge and skills.

Allowable weaknesses: Tends to contribute on a narrow front and can dwell on the technicalities.

Don't be surprised to find that: They overload you with information.

Read more about Belbin team roles at belbin.com

You should have recognised yourself in one of more of the team roles (see fworkletsplay.com for more information).

Hopefully, this has illustrated that the source of your value is far, far broader than the transferable skills you picked up in your last job. Your talents might include inspiring people, identifying the right people to hire or collaborate with, spotting mistakes, connecting people to the right information, fine-tuning things, automating, generating ideas. And it also shows that you should stop trying to be an all-rounder once and for all. Work on your strengths, work *around* your weaknesses.

Your mission must be to get into flow. Start doing more of those things that you're naturally good at – which are also the things you find most enjoyable. In addition, you will need to *stop* doing those things that are out of flow for you – by delegating them, outsourcing them or swapping skills with complementary people. Few people dare to do this and so most of us never really experience flow. We push and struggle in our work for mediocre results. Imagine only doing the things that you are great at doing and working with others who are great at the things you hate. How much more effective would you be?

Note that there is a world of difference between what you *can* do and what you're naturally great at. We have all become pretty good at a number of things through our careers and life experiences (sometimes simply through necessity), but what we are interested in here are those things that you are really *great* at and enjoy. Build a life around those and you'll be many times more successful than if you base your work on what you're simply OK at.

Write in your playbook which roles you think represent you and which strengths and weaknesses you recognise in yourself from the list above. Also write down one thing you currently do in your work that clearly feels *out of flow* for you, something that really grates with you. How could you minimise or remove this activity altogether from your work?

Find your foil

Charlie Thuillier is creator of the world's first healthy ice cream, Oppo, now stocked in thousands of stores around Europe (read the remarkable story in Secret eight).

But when he set out on his mission, he decided very quickly he needed his brother Harry to join him to make it work because as Charlie told me, "He's fantastic at what I'm bad at – we're total foils of each other."

In Belbin team roles, Charlie is primarily a Shaper and Resource investigator, which is great for someone trying to bring an innovation to the market. In his own words, "I am enthusiastic, challenging and thrive on pressure. However I can be impatient, over-optimistic, and can get bored once a project moves to the fine-tuning stage. Harry is the finisher, the optimiser. He has the perfectionist's eye on details."

Harry is primarily a Co-ordinator in Belbin terms, using his tact, insight and control to set goals and find the right people to execute them. Charlie explains, "I tend to run new pitches (and swiftly hand them over once won) and longer-term ideas for growth, while Harry looks after the team, structure, processes and makes the idea happen. Although we both run Oppo jointly we don't end up treading on each other's toes."

If you are starting a business you might well be working on your own initially, but you can hire people on a task-by-task basis as your foil. For example, a coach to help you set goals and hold you accountable, a bookkeeper to keep your accounts in order, or a project manager to help you organise a complex project. If you choose to start your business with a friend or colleague, beware making the common mistake of choosing someone exactly like you. Look instead for your foil.

Feeling uncomfortable?

The story of the human race is the story of men and women selling themselves short.

Abraham Maslow, American psychologist, 1908–70

All this talk of naming your talents and strengths might be unsettling. Perhaps this sounds like boasting to you. British culture in particular has a history of encouraging people not to sing their own praises. But unless you at least identify your talents, how can you ever get to use them? It is a generous act to know your talents and use them. Your talents are not really for you – they are for everyone else around you who benefits when you put them into action. In fact, keeping them to yourself is the selfish act.

It can be easy to overlook something you do well as a talent. It comes so naturally to you, you can't imagine not being able to do it. And you may not have noticed that other people don't have this talent. We have so bought into the idea that what we do for a living must be hard work that getting paid to do what comes naturally almost feels like cheating.

I have a friend who is an excellent flirt. He's genuinely charming and charismatic with everyone he meets. And that's a talent. I know people who make their entire living teaching other men and women how to flirt. Ask some supportive friends what talents you have that you might have missed and write them down in your playbook.

Talents, skills and passions

The sweet spot for getting paid to play is where talent, skill and passion meet. Talent is what you're born with. Great comedians have been making people laugh since their earliest school days. But when they first step up to a mic to perform they still usually 'die'. This is because pacing, audience interaction and writing material are skills that still have to be learned. The third factor is passion. Even if you're good at something, you won't excel at it unless you enjoy it. I happen to be talented and skilled at wiring extremely complex digital video systems together. It's easy for me and I had a lot of practice in it at a previous job but I'm not passionate about it, so there is no way I would make it a central part of my working life.

The fastest route to getting paid to play is to choose something that you are not just talented at and passionate about, but that you already have some knowledge and skills in. Your depth of experience is a large part of how other people value you and decide what to pay you. The problem of course is that when you make a leap into a new field that excites you, you may not have the same level of expertise in it that veterans have. And that can make it difficult to get paid what you would like.

If you choose your steps wisely, you can minimise the setback. The more of the skills you can use from previous work, the quicker you will be able to get paid for the new line of work. Even if you're moving into a completely different field, if you're using the great track record you have built, for example, in managing people or organising projects, you can still be very valuable.

Also think twice before you ditch your previous area of expertise entirely. If you have a talent for something, it may just be the form you use it in your current work that is unsatisfying. I assumed my decades of experience with technology would play no part at all in my new more creative career. But in fact it has become a unique selling point for me when I advise people on online marketing strategy for their business. My natural affinity for technology hasn't gone away but now I use it in a much more fun way – to create powerful online experiences and find dramatic shortcuts for people to launch their creative projects on to the world. What talents do you have that you could imagine enjoying using if you could just find a more interesting way to employ them? Write them down.

The great love-versus-money balancing act

It's time to make a choice of how to use your mix of talents, skills and passions. If you want to get paid to play, does this mean you have to think commercially about everything you do? In your imagined year off, there are no doubt many different activities you would like to do. Some you want to do purely for love: they seem difficult to monetise or perhaps you don't want to even try. You might not want to expose your most personal creative work to the vagaries of the market – your art, music or poetry, for instance. Some of the kinds of work you could imagine doing might be very marketable but perhaps not quite as enjoyable. Which do you choose? This is the eternal love–versus–money balancing act.

The truth is that the 'work you do for money versus work you do for the love of it' dilemma never goes away. Even people who become world famous will continue to manage their careers carefully to balance their most commercial work with their personal passions. Scarlett Johansson is one of the most talented and in-demand actors of her generation. Like similarly successful actors, however, she will alternate very commercial projects like *Avengers: Endgame* (now the number one grossing film of all time) with ones that are more experimental like *JoJo Rabbit* which made a fraction of the amount at the box office but won her an Oscar nomination.

For the rest of us, it might mean that, as a writer, you write articles in between books or do commercial copywriting – both of which can be very creative and enjoyable. As a video artist, you fund yourself by shooting corporate videos or adverts. Or if you're working on your own app, you pick up the odd coding job on upwork. com or Toptal to keep yourself going.

Whatever you choose to keep you afloat while you build your more playful life, for heaven's sake make it enjoyable. Don't make the mistake so many make of taking any low-level work, no matter how ill-fitting. There are far too many players stuck in boring temp jobs, PA positions and punishing sales roles. If the work is a terrible fit for you, you'll be so drained afterwards, you'll have no energy for the thing you really want to do. And beware the pitfall of spending months or even years creating some fall-back source of income you're not excited about when you might be better off taking the plunge and starting straight away with what you really want to do.

You might end up creating a mix of work – some more like play than others, some more financially rewarding than others – but none of it that is too far from playing. Make sure you are in *flow*, doing something that gives you some of the experience of what you truly love. Sometimes you find your more commercial work becoming symbiotic with the work you do purely for pleasure.

If you want to quit your job but you need to replace your salary straight away, you might choose a 'stepping stone' project, such as contracting, consulting or freelancing, to get you out of your current work but leave you a little more flexibility to investigate your ideas.

That's what Ernesto Moreno did and it led him into something he really loves.

You never know where your stepping stone will take you

Ernesto Moreno was a management consultant at PriceWaterhouse-Coopers when he read my first book. It inspired him to escape the 9 to 5 and become an independent business consultant. His very first client was fellow Venezuelan Gus Salguero who had started a market stall in London's Camden Town selling arepas, stuffed corn patties which are a classic Venezuelan dish but relatively unknown in Europe. Gus's food was popular and had even been featured on television but he struggled to make a profit.

Although Ernesto started as a consultant, he ended up joining Gus as business partner and together they created London's first Venezuelan restaurant, *Arepa and Co*. The restaurant was a hit and the two men decided to open a second branch, twice the size.

At first, Ernesto says, *"It was a bit chaotic. We worried for a while that perhaps we'd made a mistake opening the new branch but we managed to turn it around. Now it's very successful."*

Ernesto and Gus complement each other well. Gus's passion is still the food above all else and he is the face of the business. Ernesto is happy to mostly work behind the scenes.

> *"I've discovered through my work at Arepa and Co that my passion is creating a culture of happiness and high performance through working with teams and implementing good systems and processes.*

At the time of writing, Venezuela is going through a political and economic crisis and the Venezuelan community in London has grown enormously as a result. Arepa and Co has become a focal point for the community and as Ernesto says, *"Sometimes playing the role of the unofficial Venezuelan embassy".*

In fact, politician Juan Guaidó, recognised by 60 countries as the acting president of Venezuela, was in London recently visiting UK Prime Minister Boris Johnson and before leaving for Davos, he arranged to meet with members of the Venezuelan community in London and chose Arepa and Co as the venue to do so.

Ernesto and Gus are now considering a third branch of the restaurant and have launched the Association of Venezuelans in the UK to help Venezuelans find jobs and create a new life.

Choose the right stepping stone to get out of your job and you too could open up remarkable new opportunities.

Read more about Arepa and co at arepaandco.com

How to avoid being a starving artist (actor, musician, poet or novelist)

If you're passionate about your art, acting, music, poetry or novel-writing, you'll already be well aware of the difficulties of making a living from them. The cold, hard reality of the creative arts is that there is plenty of supply (i.e. people wanting to create) and not a huge amount of demand (people willing to pay money for what you create). This makes the arts very competitive. As a result, it's a challenge to succeed but, hey, it's a challenge to do anything really important.

You want to keep doing your art and you don't want to starve. What can you do? First off, quit the dilemma once and for all of asking "Can I continue my art?" You *are* an artist – you don't get to choose. The question now is "*How* do I continue my art?" What do you need to do in order to be able to create your art and make a living – even if the two things have to be separate at first? Think about how you will manage the development of your art over time. Let go of the idea that the choice is either to be a full-time artist or to give up. Manage your love–versus–money balance to make it work.

If you're serious about making a full-time living from your art, decide that you will do whatever it takes to make it happen. Get creative about what you produce and how you market it. If the conventions of your field are working against you, sidestep them. Model the people you respect who have succeeded in your field. Everyone says acting is very hard to make a living out of, yet some actors always have work (and they're not necessarily the most talented). How do they do it? What can you learn from them?

Get over the idea that if you just produce good work, you will magically be discovered. Realise that to make any progress, you need to put at least as much effort into promoting your work as you do making it. If you're terrible at self-promotion, find someone else to do it for you. You can sit in a garret painting for the rest of your life, but if you never tell anyone about your work, no one will ever get to enjoy it. It's remarkable the number of people I see writing music or novels who never dare show it to anyone. The creative act is incomplete without an audience. Yes, it's frightening to share your creative work and hear what could be negative feedback, but don't you dare use that as a reason to avoid it.

What's the worst that could happen? Someone might say that all your work to date is utterly worthless. They could even be right. And still, you would be an artist. It might be that you haven't found the right medium for yourself yet. Whatever it is you're trying to express through your art is still valid. Perhaps you shouldn't even be painting, you should be writing. Or if you're writing, you should be painting. Perhaps you haven't dared to go deep enough into what you're trying to express. The only thing you can do wrong is to give up the whole game.

The facts are always friendly.

Carl Rogers, American psychologist and researcher

Embrace portfolio working. Don't waste any energy on complaining – take responsibility for your own success and learn from successful artists how to make it work.

How to choose what to do next

So now you have some idea of how valuable your talents can be, what do you do with them? You might have several options in mind for where to head next, but how do you choose the right one to pursue now? Or maybe you can't seem to come up with a single viable path to take? Perhaps you've been thinking about all this for a while now. If you've been going round in circles trying to decide on your next move, you are probably stuck in 'pinball thinking'.

Here's something I've seen a lot in the participants at careers workshops. The career-changer is stuck in a job they don't enjoy but can't seem to find a new direction to move in. They are longing for someone else to tell them the magic answer of what work they should do. They believe the answer is *out there somewhere* – some job option they haven't thought of yet. And once someone shows them it, everything will drop into place.

Does this sound familiar to you? In reality, the information is within you. You've simply discounted too many options by getting into 'pinball thinking'. Just like the ball-bearing in a game of pinball, your internal dialogue about possible work options rapidly pings back and forth before falling down a hole. Does the conversation in your head sound something like the following?

I know, I could be a writer!

Oh no, I couldn't stand the isolation.

Maybe I could start my own business!

But it's too risky right now to do that.

I could try PR.

But I'd have to retrain and I don't have the money.

Ah, I'm stuck. . .

I have no idea what I want to do.

(Game over)

In reality, of course, you've had three ideas just in that one internal conversation. In each one of those ideas there is something that speaks to you. That means there is information there about the kind of work you find attractive: information that you're currently discarding.

Here's a better way of thinking. Take all your ideas for possible directions for your work, as flawed as they may be, and get them down on paper. To help with this, look back at the notes in your playbook from Secret one: the activities you would do in a year out, the things you enjoyed most in your career, the people you admire or are jealous of, the projects you would do if you couldn't fail, and the things you enjoy so much you find it difficult to stop doing them. All these answers point to what you want more of in your working life. Make a list of work options – careers, jobs, freelance roles, business ideas, or creative projects – that will give you something of the experience you really want.

If some of the activities you originally wrote down seem impossible right now (renovating a castle, sailing around the world, studying yoga in India for six months), don't throw them out just yet. This is telling you about something that you want more of in your life. What is it? Is it freedom, adventure, personal development, working in a team, having an impact on the world? Is it the experience of working with your hands, creating something new, improving something, solving a tough problem, realising a vision? What kind of work could give you some of this? Remember there is always a way to get the experience you want to have, even if it's in a different form to what you first thought of.

Write down at least three to five work options. Include the kind of work you currently do, just for comparison. Then for each option write answers to the following four questions:

➡ What is it that *appeals* about this job, business or project?

➡ What is it that's *unattractive* to me and doesn't appeal about this option?

➡ What are the practical *obstacles* that might get in the way of taking this option?

➡ What *assets* do I have in my favour for this option? Talents, skills, knowledge, experience, contacts?

For the example option of writing a book, you might write:

Appeals: Being creative, getting my ideas out into the world, having an impact and becoming famous.

Doesn't appeal: Doesn't pay very well, I might not be self-disciplined enough to write a whole book on my own.

Obstacles: I don't know anyone who could get me published and my spelling is really bad.

Assets: I've written a couple of articles and people have said they're good. I really enjoy putting my ideas down on paper. My friend knows a literary agent. I think I've got a good topic.

Then repeat this process for at least a couple of other options, writing out the answers to the four questions for each one.

Now you've got all your imperfect options laid out in front of you, instead of throwing them away, you can start to address the problem areas. How could you minimise the part of this option that doesn't appeal? For the writing example, perhaps you could co-write something or create your book by transcribing talks to an audience.

Then look at the obstacles and brainstorm ways around them. In the writing example, who do you know who could put you in contact with someone in the publishing world? Is there an event you could go to where you could meet a publisher? Could you use spell-check software to get round your problem with spelling?

When you've worked on all the downsides of each option, take a fresh look at the list. Even if you still have practical concerns, which one of these options is most exciting to you? What's the part that's most exciting about it? How can you have that exciting part, while minimising the unappealing part and sidestepping the obstacles? Remember from the last Secret that there is always a way to have the part you want most, even if you have to use some seriously lateral thinking to find a way to get it.

Now look at the common themes emerging in the 'What appeals about this' column. What does this tell you about the kind of work that is attractive to you right now? Are there other ways you could get this appealing part? As you think of more options to explore, add them to your notes. Is there some way to combine several of your desirable options into a new one? If so, put that new option down. Come back to your notes over the next few days and weeks and add new ideas as they come to you. Don't try and work it all out in one sitting.

You can download editable worksheets to fill in for this exercise from fworkletsplay.com

Which of these options do you want to investigate first? You're not committing to changing your whole career. You're just choosing which to look into a bit more deeply. Mark your two or three favourite options. You can research all of them but for now, pick one of these favourites to look at first.

As a player, there really is no single career that is the ultimate answer for you. Your career is something you play out by testing, exploring, experimenting and experiencing. As you get clearer and clearer where you want to head next, you adjust your course to move closer to getting paid to play.

Take the Sunday Night test

It's important to check that the path you're choosing to explore further is something you are genuinely interested in and you're not just following the expectations that others have of you. Imagine it's Sunday night. Tomorrow, Monday morning, you are starting this new work life you have chosen from your list. How do you feel? Are you excited? Maybe a little bit scared? Good! Or are you just feeling flat, resigned? Change the details of this option until you can imagine looking forward to doing it.

If all else fails, toss a coin. If you can't decide between two or more directions you could choose, try tossing a coin. At the moment you discover the result, check in quickly with how you feel. Are you secretly a little bit disappointed or a little bit excited? Find a way to do the one that excites you.

If you're still stuck, choose anything on the list. If you've been stuck in the grip of a career crisis for some time, it's common to end up in a state of mild to moderate depression (even if you haven't identified it as such yet). This is not a very resourceful state for building a new life. So choosing to engage in anything you enjoy is a good thing to do. It makes you a little happier and it reconnects you with your passion and creativity. And you need these to make changes in your life. That's why people often find doing something enjoyable but quite unrelated to their work (e.g. joining a choir, starting an evening class) seems to unlock them and enable them to move on.

In Secret three you will find out how to get started right away on exploring one of the options on your list.

Put it into play

Keys to this secret:

➡ Get into flow: maximise your moment of magic, work on your strengths, work around your weaknesses. This will bring you far greater success in much less time.

➡ Get others to tell you strengths you might be taking for granted.

➡ Stop pinball thinking and lay out all your options to assess.

What you should have now:

➡ An idea of your moment of magic, the strengths used and the impact it has on others.

➡ Some idea of what being in flow looks like for you.

➡ A shortlist of options to investigate further and a favourite to start with.

Take ten minutes to play:

➡ Go and experience your moment of magic. Find a way to do that thing you're naturally good at which people get a lot of value from. Call someone up now and offer to do this for free for them if necessary.

Exclusive extras on fworkletsplay.com:

➡ More information on personality types and how to take the test.

➡ Editable worksheets for you to download and fill in to solve your pinball thinking and choose what to do next.

Secret three
How to get started right now

There are no rules or formulas for success. You just have to live it and do it. Knowing this gives us enormous freedom to experiment toward what we want. Believe me, it's a crazy, complicated journey. It's trial and error. It's opportunism. It's quite literally, 'Let's try lots of this stuff and see how it works.'

Dame Anita Roddick 1942–2007, founder of The Body Shop

You should now have some idea of the talents you have to offer and a shortlist of options of how to put them to use. In this Secret we'll look at how to put it all into action right away and launch your journey to get paid to play. In order to do that, you'll need to embrace a new, more playful way of approaching work that does away with five-year plans and long-term goals. If you can do that, you might be surprised – and delighted – at just where your work ends up taking you, as young entrepreneurs Sam Bompas and Harry Parr have discovered.

Playing with food

When I spoke to Sam Bompas and Harry Parr ten years ago they had been creating their remarkable experiments with food and drink for a couple of years. Those early days were marked by fun and innovative projects that often required Sam and Harry to think on their feet.

As Harry explains . . .

We had started playing around with jelly and making high-end desserts that could be moulded into complex shapes. We were spotted with our jellies at a festival and were featured in a very small piece in The Sunday Times' *Style magazine announcing that "Jelly is making a comeback!" They listed our website which at the time was ridiculously basic and featured a logo we'd drawn ourselves with a pencil.*

People started contacting us and one of the first projects came about with a phone call from Warwick Castle asking us to make a giant model of the castle out of jelly. We realised that what they wanted was physically impossible so Sam somehow decided that what they really wanted was a 12-course Victorian breakfast and not this giant jelly. And amazingly they decided to commission this breakfast. So we went from a project about jelly to being commissioned to do an elaborate 12-course feast. We had pitched the food that they served to Queen Victoria when she was at the castle. So, we wondered how we were going to do this and pull it all together. And at the time I was training to become an architect so I thought the only way to do it was just to draw a plan. We went into the utmost detail about how everything was going to be served and we ended up doing choreography for all of the servants so that every part of the meal could be served at exactly the right time.

And then we instructed our friends, who we dressed up as Victorian servants and butlers, that as long as they followed exactly what was on this little drawing that we had, that everything would be fine. And it all worked out really well at the end.

And that's when we realised that we could pitch just about anything and work out quite quickly afterwards how we're going to do it. We can always make it work by the time it all happens.

Today Bompas & Parr is a 20-person company that has created remarkable flavour experiences in almost every continent. 80% of its work is international and it has worked with both cultural institutions like London's V&A Museum and San Francisco's Museum of Modern Art and global brands like Coca Cola, Mercedes and Vodafone. Its projects have included a breathable gin and tonic, the world's first vegan hotel suite for Hilton, the world's lightest dessert, the world's largest cake, and 250,000 people experiencing flavoured fireworks in London on New Year's Eve. Bompas & Parr have published six books and recently founded the British Museum of Food.

Looking back over the past ten years, Sam told me recently,

"I've had a thoroughly thrilling decade getting paid to do what I relish. And we now generate even more ideas than ever because we have all the creative connections between the people in the company. I feel like we have another 10,000 ideas for projects we haven't even started yet.

Sam also has a message for you and the other readers of this book:

"The premise of what John writes about is even more relevant now because the barriers to entry are lower. Today it is much much easier to share what you're doing and what you're excited about and help other people find it. There's no excuse!"

Find out more about Bompas & Parr at bompasandparr.com

Most of the players I have interviewed, including Bompas & Parr, are fully engaged in an exciting process of playing out their work but couldn't say where it will take them in five years' time. And they certainly didn't plan to create an international flavour studio and be named a top ten influencer in the global food scene when they first started playing with jelly. This is a very different approach to careers from what most of us have been taught and yet it works.

Myth 6: I can't start anything until I know exactly where I'm heading

Today, there is little point picking some goal far off in the distance and expecting to be able to follow a well-planned path to get you there – things are moving too damn fast and life never turns out the way you expect it to anyway. Aside from that, each step you take positions you at a different place with a different view and different choices. There's no way to predict in advance what opportunities will present themselves and how you'll feel about them once you're there. Be willing to play it out, choose your next step because you really want to do it for its own merits – even if you can't see how it might fit with a conventional career path or other people's view of success.

As my friend, Mark, said when he saw me reading a careers book, "Why do you bother? Don't worry about a career, just pick an interesting project and go do it. And when you've done that one, see where it's landed you and pick the next one." This process led to him becoming an expert in his field (teaching English as a foreign language), travelling all over the world and setting up his own English school in Vietnam.

Beware the 'good career move' or the business chosen purely for the financial rewards. This is not the route to a happy life. Billionaire Warren Buffett was once asked for careers advice by an MBA student. The student thought he should go work in finance for a while just to make money then do what he really wanted to later. The billionaire thought this was a ridiculous idea, and said, "That's like saving sex for old age." Besides, it's very difficult to get rich by doing something you don't enjoy. You can't excel at something when your heart isn't in it.

Two of my best career moves were instinctual and turned out very well. Straight out of college, I joined a tiny software start-up of three people which went on to become one of the best-known names in their industry, creating systems to automate TV stations all over the world. Then I moved to a small start-up making special effects software. The week I joined they were bought by the biggest name in the business. This led to me having an extremely impressive CV without any deliberate planning.

So was I just lucky? Perhaps not. Even if I couldn't describe my criteria at the time, I was joining early-stage companies with smart people doing very original work. And smart people doing very original work often go on to become industry-leading companies (or get bought by them). When later I joined a 'Big 5' consultancy because it seemed a 'good career move', I gained an impressive job title but I was miserable.

Developing a commercial sense of what will sell well in the market is very helpful, but while you are doing that you'll find that pursuing the projects you enjoy and that feel important to you now is more likely to lead to success and financial riches than plotting for some far-off end-goal and making compromising 'good career moves' along the way.

The problem with goals

But shouldn't you at least set some goals? If you've ever worked with a coach or read a book about success, you've probably been advised to set lots of goals. Setting financial targets and some other goals can be helpful (particularly as an entrepreneur) but beware getting obsessed with them.

Let's face it, if goals were so powerful, a lot more people would reach them – and everyone who did would be happy. There are a number of problems with this incessant goal-setting. It places a focus on the future and suggests relentless action and compromise in the present to get there. When you achieve that goal, you allow yourself a brief period of rejoicing and then set a new one. Ugh! I can feel the existential desolation just writing that. It's all very mesomorphic, by which I mean action-focused. What about how you want to *be* or *feel* from moment to moment?

There's no goal you can tick off for that.

Myth 7: Once my life is the way I want it to be, then I'll be happy

Your goals won't make you happy. The truth is it's not anything in the future that will make you happy but how you live *today*, how you choose to create this day of your life. Even getting rich is no guarantee of happiness. Research shows that when people win the lottery, they have a short-lived boost in happiness and then settle back to roughly the level of happiness they had before.

It's not your success that will create your happiness. It's your happiness that will create your success. And you can't create happiness in the future by consistently creating misery in your life now. If you can't create what you want in some form today, it's likely you will never have it. I'm sure you've seen the kind of person who is always running faster and faster in the hope of creating a more relaxed future and of course never gets there.

> *Most people treat the present moment as if it were an obstacle that they need to overcome. Since the present moment is Life itself, it is an insane way to live.*

> **Eckhart Tolle, author of *The Power of Now***

The healthier alternative is to create a good present that grows into a great future. Set some goals if you find them helpful but then turn your focus from the far-off to the present day and create some of the experience of your dream life in the here and now – even if it's scaled down to start with. Play out the unfolding of your life's work. Pick a project that will give you more of what you want – and start it right away.

When you focus on getting into flow today – doing what you enjoy and what comes naturally to you – you'll be amazed at just how fast you'll find yourself progressing.

The problem with thinking

Thinking is overrated. And most of us do far too much of it. Successful people apparently have fewer thoughts – they don't engage in endless deliberation. Perhaps this is because the research shows that over-thinking makes you miserable and unmotivated.

Over thinking (i.e. rumination) ushers in a host of adverse conse-quences: It sustains or worsens sadness, fosters negatively-biased think-ing, impairs a person's ability to solve problems, saps motivation, and interferes with concentration and initiative.

Sonja Lyubomirsky, *The How of Happiness*

If you're truly stuck in your life and can't seem to move forward, chances are you're thinking too much. A lot of people who turn up at careers workshops are stuck in the thinking trap. I know it well: I've wasted years there myself. It's the belief that if we sit and think about something for long enough, the light will shine down from above and we'll find some new answer not available to us before. Unfortunately, this very rarely happens. Why do we even think it would? If you've thought about a problem for five minutes and not found the solution, more time spent sitting alone thinking without any new input is very unlikely to bring fresh insights.

I guess it's school that taught us that thinking was the solution – if you don't have the answer at first, think harder. This might work for a maths problem but it doesn't work very well for life decisions.

The problem is that we think within our own limits of what we know and what we believe is possible. Career problems are very rarely problems of external limitation. They are more usually a reflection of the limits of our knowledge and beliefs.

The solution? Stop thinking and start playing. Here's how to do it.

Pick a play project

It's time to stop trying to find the perfect answer for what to do with your life, and start today doing something you really want to do. Look at the shortlist of options you produced in the last Secret and the one that you marked out as most exciting to investigate first.

What small project could you start straight away that will launch you into this line of work, or at least allow you to try it out? This is your first play project. It should be something you can do in a few weeks or a couple of months. You may have already had a taste of this activity in your first experiment with Play Wednesday as explained in Secret one. The point now is to define something that will give you a tangible result and with a clear end-point. If this is a new activity for you and you're not sure how much you'll enjoy it, choose something small enough that you can finish before you get bored. Break it down if it's currently too large.

'Find a happy person, and you will find a project'

Happiness researcher Sonja Lyubomirsky writes in her book *The How of Happiness*: People who strive for something significant, whether it's learning a new craft or raising moral children, are far happier than those who don't have strong dreams or aspirations. Find a happy person and you will find a project.

The content of your project will depend on what stage you are at in your search. If you're still weighing up possible options, your project should help you explore and experience this option. If you've already got some idea where you want to head to, this project should launch you right into doing it.

How to choose your project

Don't obsess about choosing the perfect project to do. It doesn't have to represent the future direction of your entire life. It's simply to give you an experience of one of the options you chose in the last Secret. The point is to get into motion. You can always correct your course on the fly.

Make sure to choose something that is likely to be enjoyable to do, not just for the result. The bottom line is if it didn't give you the results you hoped for and doesn't make you rich, would you still be glad you did it?

Aim for a project that will give you an experience of being in flow, perhaps centred on something you know is a moment of magic for you. But bear in mind that the best projects are a step up for you and might be a bit scary to take on. We'll see later how to manage your anxiety about taking on new challenges.

If it's something that calls to you right now and you think you'd enjoy doing it, go for it. If it will take you somewhere interesting or you will learn something in the process that will be useful to you for subsequent projects, then all the better.

The project you choose will depend on where you are right now in your shift from worker to player. Here are three specific options for common situations.

If you're in career paralysis

If you've got completely stuck on what to do with your career, almost any project you feel excited about will have the benefit of getting you moving again. Don't worry too much about how it might lead to making a living. You can focus on making money or progressing your move with later projects (Secret five will help you with this). The main thing for you is to get into play and indulge yourself by becoming immersed in something you'll really enjoy. And if all you do is learn more about what you like (and don't like) and what you're good at (and weak at), that is very valuable in itself.

I meet people all the time who long to be, for example, a writer but have been deliberating whether it's possible for them. If you want to be a writer, grab a pen and paper and start writing. Congratulations, you're now a writer. If you've been dabbling with writing for a while now, make your project to enter a writing competition, or to write an article to get published somewhere. Even if you don't end up making a career out of writing, you will have had the experience of doing it and will have learned what that's like for you. You'll probably also have come up with a few new ideas of what to try next.

Whatever you choose, you're likely to learn reusable skills even if your next project is completely different – skills such as how to ask people for help, how to collaborate, how to keep going when you feel stuck and how to manage your motivation, creativity and time. You'll also get to experience your own ability to manifest something that you want in your life. This is a wonderful thing in itself if you've been feeling powerless about improving your work situation.

If you're self-employed

If you're already self-employed, use your project to open up a new line of business that's closer to your heart, that keeps you in flow, and that feels more like play. Think about the pieces of work you have done in the past that you have most enjoyed. How could you run a campaign to focus on winning more of exactly that kind of work now? It's surprising how few people do this. You could also use your play project to open another channel of contact with your target market such as a YouTube channel, using Instagram, or starting a live event. Or you might use it as your first foray into creating an online offer that can make you money without you turning up (more on this later).

If you need to make some cash quickly in your existing business

If you already have a business or work for yourself but need a quick cash injection before doing anything else, make your play project to run a cash-generating campaign. Go back to your favourite clients or customers and find out where they are and what their needs are now. See if you can offer them something new to address it. Your easiest source of sales is always from people who have already worked with you and enjoyed the experience.

Alternatively, you could run a referral competition. Approach everyone who has worked for you and ask if they can name two or more people who need what you offer. Make it fun and send a present such as a bottle of champagne to everyone who sends you a referral. Give a prize to the person who sends you the most referrals.

If you're moving into a completely new field

If you're looking to enter a completely new line of work, use your project as a chance to immerse yourself in it and start exploring. Here's how:

1. Start to live this new line of work. Read books about it and autobiographies of leaders in this field. Follow your favourite leaders and experts on social media and share a curated feed of what you find out.

2. Get in the mix. Go to exhibitions and conferences. Go out to networking meetings, talks and workshops. Talk to others and learn what's hot in this part of the world.

3. Take any chance you can to experience doing the kind of work you're interested in, even if unpaid to start with.

Once you know the field you want to enter, if you're aiming to land a job rather than go self-employed, choose a play project that could get you noticed by possible employers: interview thought leaders in this area for your own podcast, or help out at an exhibition or conference.

Even faster than Google

Myth 8: I should go and research this all day on the internet

You might be thinking that the best way to find out about a new field you want to work in is to go and research it thoroughly on the internet. A certain amount of reading around is important but beware of getting drawn into an endless process of research sitting at your computer. It's a huge time-sink and doesn't really show you what it's like to work in this field. Career decisions ultimately cannot be made with rational thinking alone, they must *feel* right – and research will only take you so far.

Beware in particular using 'research' as a way to systematically discount the career paths you are really excited about. If you go looking for evidence that something is impossible, you'll find it.

Instead, look for the people who made it work and follow their example.

Once you've researched the basics, here's something even faster than Google. Think of a key question you need the answer to – something that could move you forward significantly. Then find someone who could answer it for you: someone who is actually doing the kind of work you're interested in. Try to choose someone who is successful at it and enjoys it. You'll be amazed just what you can find out in ten minutes speaking to someone knowledgeable. Most people will be quite happy to help you by talking about their work for ten minutes.

Here's how to approach it.

➡ Decide what's the one question you would most like an answer to right now. Be specific so it's easy to answer. Don't ask, "What's llama farming like?" Say, "I want to get into llama farming, so can you tell me what your typical day looks like? What are the best parts and the worst parts?" Don't ask the basic stuff you can find on the internet, focus on asking about the things that come from real-world experience.

➡ Who do you know who might be able to answer your question? If you can't think of anyone, who do you know that might know someone who can? We all know as many as 200 people. By asking friends to ask their friends and colleagues, you immediately access 40,000 people.

Use what you find out in your ongoing research and when you're ready, think of your next question to ask.

Wanted: chemical explosives expert

Sam Bompas of Bompas & Parr told me that in one of their first projects,

We created a breathable cocktail. We vaporised gin and tonic to make a cocktail cloud that filled a building. If you're in there for 40 minutes you have the equivalent of a strong G&T.

This project had considerable health and safety risks:

If you vaporise spirits the resulting fog is extremely flammable. We got in touch with a leading chemical explosives expert and asked him to get involved with the project. We didn't have any budget for consultancy work but he thought it sounded like fun and answered our question "How much alcohol can you vaporise before it becomes an explosive risk?"

If you put the hours in you're going to be able to speak to the right person. You can always find people that know more than you. You just need to track them down.

70,000 people have now experienced Bompas & Parr's breathable G&T.

Today their company of 20 includes creatives, cooks, mixologists, specialised technicians, project managers, producers and film-makers and they contract externally with structural engineers, scientists, artists and psychologists. So while they now approach projects in a more formalised way, they still know they can find out anything they need for a project.

Think big, start small

Have you got a grand vision for a business or a creative project? Or are you just wondering how to take your first steps? The key is to break your ideas down into something small enough to be manageable. Here are some quickfire examples.

If you want to a write a book, you could start writing your ideas out as a blog and assemble them later into a book. I started writing a blog to experiment with my ideas about getting paid to play and this led to the book you're reading right now.

If you want to create an online course you could sketch out what you want to cover, run it as a three-week programme in a

Facebook group for free or a reduced price the first time and deliver the content live each week as an online presentation. This way you get to test out your material and get feedback about what people value in it and where they get lost. Unless you are already very experienced at running online programmes or have a large following, this is a much better way to create something for the first time than building it out as a do-it-yourself course online. You can read more about how to create a successful online course in Secret seven.

If you want to sell goods or trade international crafts, start on eBay, move on to your own eBay shop and then you might graduate to your own website. If you're making your own handmade crafts, go to etsy.com or a similar site to sell them.

If you already have your own business but want to nudge it towards something that feels more playful to you, choose a project that will explore a new, more enjoyable, income stream. Look for that sweet spot of doing something you really enjoy and you're great at but which fulfils a need your customers recognise they have. You'll know when you're on track as you'll find you attract interest quickly.

Artists, turn your home into a gallery. London photographer Julian Bolt was encouraged by his wife Sonia and his men's group to hold the first exhibition of his work. Since he didn't have access to a gallery he held it in his small basement flat in an unfashionable part of London. He and Sonia stayed up late for many nights, clearing up the flat, printing his images and mounting them on the walls. He received plenty of positive feedback from the constant stream of visitors and sold nearly £3,000 of photos. One of the visitors was a gallery owner. She agreed to give Julian his own exhibition in her beautiful art gallery in the heart of London's gallery quarter. His next exhibition after that was in a Parisian gallery.

Want to launch a regular event? For five years I ran a monthly London event called Scanners Night for creative people who want to do lots of different projects. It often sold out and was featured in multiple newspapers and magazines. But the evening started as a free meet-up of six people at a London bar. One of those six was a friend and one was a client. The rest I found by posting a notice on a bulletin board for scanners. You can do the same thing for your own event.

Pick a date and a venue (which could simply be a café or bar), find out where the people you want to invite hang out and tell them. You might also put a listing on Meetup.com or craigslist. You can base the first event around a particular topic of discussion or give a brief talk yourself, or meet at an interesting exhibition. Act like an entrepreneur and do everything you can to get people to turn up for the first few events. Be willing to personally email, call or message people to get enough people in the room. Commit to making it happen. If you're worried you might be sitting on your own all night, call a couple of friends to come along. The worst-case scenario then is that you spend a pleasant night talking with your friends. Grow your event into a regular thing and you could start charging people to attend.

Want to change the world? Take a tip from Mohammed Yunus, creator of the Grameen Bank which pioneered microloans to some of the poorest people in the world. In 1976 Professor Yunus loaned $27 out of his own pocket to 42 women in a village in Bangladesh. The women were making furniture and were forced to pay all their profits to loan sharks for the bamboo they used as raw material. The tiny sum allowed the women to pay off the loans and start to pull themselves out of poverty. Today, Grameen Bank has 2,600 branches, over 9 million borrowers and has loaned over $20 billion with a 99% repayment rate. Yunus and the Grameen Bank were awarded the Nobel Peace Prize in 2006.

POWER-UP: Take the 30-day challenge

What can you do as a project in just a few weeks that will set you on the path to your grand vision? I ran a programme for several years called The Ideas Lab 30 Day Challenge with up to 300 people around the world taking part at a time, daring to create something they care about and put it out into the world in 30 days. What I discovered is that this 30-day timeframe is ideal for creating something tangible without getting lost in the detail. The key is to not to just research and explore but to actually produce something you can share with people. That turns what could be a theoretical exercise into a real entrepreneurial adventure. And it's exactly how all the entrepreneurs featured in this book operate.

Now it's your turn. Using the above examples as inspiration, write down your larger objective and then sketch out a small project you can do in 30 days that allows you to take your first step. Then put perfectionism aside and dive into it.

Some of my entrepreneurial clients hate the idea of starting their business in this incremental way. They believe they should go for the big splash and launch with a fabulous website and branding from day one.

This is OK if you have a couple of successful ventures under your belt already or you have the money to do formal market research, but it's a bad idea for those of us just starting out. Why? Right now as you begin your business or creative project, you think you know what it's going to be, but the truth is you don't. As soon as it's exposed to the atmosphere, it changes. When you put your idea out into the world, it morphs and evolves as you interact with the potential market or audience. It must if you want to create something successful.

Matt Mullenweg, creator of WordPress, which now powers over 75 million websites said, "You can never fully anticipate how an audience is going to react to something you've created until it's out there. That means every moment you're working on something without it being in the public it's actually dying, deprived of the oxygen of the real world."

Even if you happen to have a great idea, you might not realise where the real value is in it. You might design a brand at an early stage that's all about how your product has a cool design but you might discover that people buy it because it saves them the expense of buying a higher priced alternative. Even big companies get it wrong sometimes. When the mobile networks enabled text messaging, they expected it to be used simply as a replacement for a pager but text messages now outnumber calls with over 23 billion messages sent each day.

Get your idea out there and evolve it on the fly.

Kick off your play project

Begin somewhere; you cannot build a reputation on what you intend to do.

Liz Smith, columnist

Start on your project as soon as you can. Why not now? Even if you only have ten minutes right now, feeling you've made a start will make a big difference to your motivation. If you have no time now, take out your diary and make an appointment with yourself in the next few days to start (we'll look more at managing your time in the next Secret). When you're ready, ask yourself what task you could do in the time you have available that would make the biggest impact on your project and begin it.

Use Play Wednesday as a day to carve out some time for your play project and start to move your working week a little closer to your vision of a year out. Having set days or times when you work on your play project also makes it far more likely you will make a habit of it.

Commit to your play project. Don't just dabble. Have you got into the habit of fiddling with lots of things but dropping them before they reach a conclusion and before anyone else gets to benefit from them? As I've said, the creative act is incomplete without an audience. How many pieces of writing sit languishing in drawers? How many songs remain only in the singer's head? How many business ideas have never been shared for fear of someone stealing them? Don't be one of those that as Henry David Thoreau said, 'Go to the grave with the song still in them'.

Follow through on your project until it's done. Create something tangible and share it with the world. The sharing could be as simple as playing your finished music to a friend, talking your initial business idea over with an expert and perhaps sharing what you discover online, emailing the description of your ideal job to everyone you know, or creating a series of interviews with people in the area that fascinates you and releasing them as a podcast.

When you're not used to finishing things, you may not realise how much there is to learn by doing so. That last 10% you need to do to finish your project is actually 50% of the work. At the point you realise you are going to share the output of your project, you are forced to round off the rough edges and make sure it's in a form that others will appreciate. It's also in the sharing that much of the learning takes place – you have to marshal your nerves to make your work public and dare to hear the feedback.

Decide how you will share the results of your project and set a date to do it. Write this down now in your diary as your *release date*. Also put it in a place you will see every day so you don't forget. Then arrange this date in advance. Let the people you'll be sharing your project with know now. This will help keep you focused. You can always renegotiate it if you absolutely have to.

Plan now how you will celebrate reaching your release date and completing your project. If you march on without acknowledging what you've done, you reduce your motivation for reaching your release date next time around. What will you do to treat yourself? Take a day off, go for a celebratory meal, treat yourself to a massage, or buy some gadget you've been longing to own? Write this in your diary next to your release date.

For some projects, it is not possible to predict when you will complete it; for instance, winning your first piece of self-employed work. You can still be clear in advance though how you will celebrate it and it can be useful to estimate how long you expect it to take.

The benefits of being in play

When you finally stop sitting around thinking and get into motion, wonderful things happen. First, you get lots of feedback – both internal and external. The external feedback is about what you're good at and not so good at and what people value most about what you're doing. The internal feedback is how it felt, what you enjoyed and what you didn't. Record it all in your playbook.

The other thing is that once you're in motion, the view is completely different. Just like the view is different for the person who gets on the train compared to the person who stays behind on the platform and watches it leave. You can try to imagine what it's like in the next town all you like but far better to get on the damn train and find out!

In transit, all sorts of opportunities present themselves that aren't visible when you're sitting at home researching on Google. You run into people who can help you on your project, you get recommendations for books you can read and websites you can use, and people ask you to help them with their projects. You might even make some money or get a job offer before you've really tried to.

Having a project you're committed to gives you definition, direction, a mission. And having a mission is attractive. Like me, you've probably met people who say, "Well, I'd quite like to do x but then again I also might do y." Your attitude towards them is very different from that with someone who says, "I'm creating this event that's happening in a month's time." You're much more likely to be able to offer helpful contacts or advice to the latter person. The clearer the purpose of your project and the more committed you are to it, the more you'll find that people step forward to help you.

Remember, when you find yourself in a café enjoying writing or you have a moment when you know you've really enjoyed helping someone, or when you've created a piece of code that works like a charm and people are using it live on the web, take a moment to appreciate it. Because as soon as you are in play, you've already arrived. You've created some of the life you wanted. Yes, it might be making you very little or no money. Yes, it might not be the perfect experience, and yes, it might have been a stressful ride to get here. Put the 'buts' aside for a moment and appreciate what you do have. It might take a while before your play turns into something that makes you money or gives you the status you'd like, but if you're having fun along the way, you will at least be enjoying the journey.

A moment of play

When I very first escaped the world of jobs and went freelance, I approached a company who were doing very cool work in music software. They hired me to write a program for an exhibit to be placed in the prestigious London Science Museum. I cycled across town to meet them at their office: a converted warehouse on the South Bank of the River Thames. The founder greeted me warmly at the door and led me into a workspace packed with elaborate electronic instruments.

We sat down with a coffee and talked over how we could represent digital sound in a way that even children at a museum could grasp. We talked about waveforms and physics and brainstormed funky ways of displaying it all. When we'd finished, I left and cycled along the South Bank just as the sun was beginning to set over St Paul's Cathedral. I realised that this was an important moment representing the life I had always wanted. I was no longer working, I was playing.

Now imagine this: what if everyone stopped waiting and hoping for their dreams to come true and simply started a project that will get them a little closer to living their dream life in the here and now? Wouldn't that be a better world to live in?

In the next Secret you'll find out how to cope with the ups and downs of getting paid to play and how you can guarantee that you get there in the end.

Put it into play

Keys to this secret:

➡ Don't worry for the moment about career plans and long-term goals. Play out your unfolding work direction.

➡ Choose a project to try out your favourite work option from the last Secret and start it straight away.

➡ Whatever grand vision you may have, find a way to break it down into something you can start now.

➡ Set a release date for your project, decide how you will share the results with others, and plan to celebrate when you get there!

What you should have now:

➡ A play project defined and a release date.

Take ten minutes to play:

➡ Start right now. Put the book down, and take ten minutes to
start on your play project. Whatever your project is, you'll be
surprised at what you can achieve in ten focused, uninter-
rupted minutes. Grab the nearest piece of paper and sketch
out your idea, or start writing, go create a Facebook group to
gather people interested in your idea, or call someone who can
help you.

Exclusive extras on fworkletsplay.com:

➡ More about Sam and Harry of Bompas & Parr talking about
how they started their remarkable business around food.

Secret four
How to guarantee your success

Life is an ongoing process of choosing between safety (out of fear and need for defence) and risk (for the sake of progress and growth). Make the growth choice a dozen times a day.

Abraham Maslow, American psychologist, 1908–70

You've now seen how to start a project that will take you one step closer to getting paid to play. Hopefully you've also taken a few minutes to actually begin it. Now let's make this really clear: there is always a way to get the experience you really want in your work. If you're flexible about how you get it, and you're willing to start working on it without knowing exactly where you're heading, you are guaranteed to get it if you simply don't stop.

Creating the world's first healthy ice cream

Brothers Harry and Charlie Thuillier are founders of Oppo, the world's first healthy ice cream. The idea for an indulgent but healthy dessert came to them out of desperation.

Harry explains:

> *We first read* Screw Work, Let's Play *while on a beach in Egypt on a windsurfing trip in 2011. It got both of us thinking about ways to do what we enjoyed doing. We got the idea to go on an adventure in Brazil.*

We decided we were going to break the unofficial world record for the longest distance travelled by kite buggy on land, unsupported. We got the sponsorship in June, and we were on a plane to Brazil by July!

But, Charlie says:

To be honest we hadn't planned everything all that well. During our kite buggy adventure we ran out of food. We started losing weight fast – not to be recommended and fairly painful!

We were surrounded by wild superfoods – fruit and vegetables growing on trees and on bushes around us. We started asking locals what we could eat and they told us what was safe. It tasted amazing – and it kept us going better than the stuff we'd originally packed. I remember eating açaí in a bowl that tasted like soft serve ice cream. We thought 'Why can't we have food like this all the time?'

I started thinking about indulgent food that tastes amazing but is good for you. What if we could create luxury ice cream that's good for you? There had been no significant innovation in ice creams for 20 years.

So I quit my job and founded Oppo. Everyone said it was ridiculous. Someone at Unilever told me it had spent £25 million trying to make healthy ice cream and failed. But that just motivated me more.

It took 25 months of research, three different factories and lots of 'head in hands' moments. We replaced sugar and cream with stevia leaf and virgin coconut oil. Each flavour is boosted with a unique superfood, creating a delicious luxury ice cream containing fewer calories than an apple. Our mission was – and still is – to free people to indulge without compromising on health, planet or flavour.

During this time I lived on very little and sofa-surfed. I slept on Harry's sofa for nine months. I managed to find the best people to work with. Landor, the branding company that normally works with companies like Apple, Kellogg's and British Airways agreed to brand us for free.

I also wangled a free desk in their office. What they didn't know is that I actually slept underneath that desk in those early days. They had showers and it saved me the time and money of commuting.

All my money was going into creating test batches of Oppo. I remember at one point looking in my account and I had £1.05 left to my name. But I was excited to create something that hadn't existed before. I felt like I was playing and couldn't wait to get to work every day.

Of course, there are times you feel like giving up, times you can't see a way forward, times it feels like the world is against you. These come thick and fast in a start-up and it's bloody hard at times but the grit and determination needed to create something is much easier to come by when you want to do whatever you're doing for the right reasons, often intrinsic motivators rather than extrinsic.

When we finally had the ice cream working I wanted to get it into Waitrose as I thought it would be more flexible than some of the bigger supermarkets. I needed to speak directly to the Waitrose ice cream buyer because otherwise getting a meeting through the usual routes would take a year. So I called up head office and said, "The ice cream buyer just called me and left a message but their name was inaudible so can you please help me out?". The receptionist gave the name and then I put the phone down. Then I called straight back, got a different receptionist and told them that the named ice cream buyer had left a message but I couldn't hear their number properly. They told me the number – and now I had my way in.

Oppo launched in Waitrose and online retailer Ocado in 2014, followed by Wholefoods and many independents. Today Harry and Charlie work at their own Oppo office with 17 others. Oppo is available in over 6,000 supermarkets across 12 countries and is growing 50% year on year.

Oppo has won four Great Taste awards and numerous other accolades. (I ate half a tub of Oppo while interviewing Harry and Charlie and can confirm it tastes fantastic.)

Read more about Oppo Ice Cream at oppobrothers.com

Welcome to the rollercoaster

Fasten your seatbelt because you're going on a rollercoaster ride. Once you set off on this journey it is far from smooth running. When you finally dare to admit what you really want and go after it, you will be giving up the constant flatline of mild discontent so many people spend their lives in. You will be *living*, not just existing. You will have fantastic highs as you achieve something you didn't even think possible. And you'll also have real lows when you get a big setback– someone important rejects your idea or says something very critical.

You'll find it easier if you can remember to decouple your self-esteem from your outcomes – and from your bank balance. Instead, feel proud of yourself when you meet your promises to yourself and others and when you manage to do something that scares you, whatever the results you get.

If you're used to living by the adage, 'Don't get your hopes up', I invite you to do the opposite. *Do* get your hopes up – dare to dream that you can have what you want. And, yes, if you hit a big setback, it will hurt. This is normal. Take a moment to lick your wounds, talk it over with friends, then keep on marching. There's always another way to get the experience you really want. In fact, these setbacks are your friends. Most people give up at the first obstacle and that means less competition for you. The only thing you can do wrong is to stop.

Having positive expectations has been shown in most situations to bring better results than expecting the worst. It's no coincidence that most successful entrepreneurs are optimists. And it's also suggested that appreciating what's already working in your life has greater benefits than obsessing about what's not working. This idea has received a lot of airplay from believers in the law of attraction, but is this really a law of physics or just wishful thinking?

The law of attraction, as made famous in the book and film *The Secret*, is a principle that states that what you think about the most tends to be attracted into your life. Think about good things – money, possessions, good relationships – and you attract those good things. Think about bad things – debt, illness, conflict – and you attract those bad things. Is it true? Is there really some mystical force or universal law of physics that gives you more of what you focus on?

The fact is that some of what's described as the law of attraction definitely operates but you don't need to believe in anything mystical to understand it. There are a number of very practical reasons our thoughts become self-fulfilling prophecies.

One of the reasons for this is that, as you may know, the majority of what we communicate to the outside world is actually done so through non-verbal communication (such as body language and tone of voice) rather than words. If you go to a networking meeting in a good state of mind, with a genuine smile on your face and relaxed, open body language, it's likely you'll connect more easily with people than if you turn up miserable, pessimistic and expecting people to ignore you. And if you spend too much time complaining, you tend to attract other people who complain and turn off others. (This doesn't mean, however, that you should become one of those people that pretend they never have a moment of disappointment or despondency.)

Another reason for the powerful effects of a positive outlook is that your brain is continually filtering the mass of information that comes into your senses according to what your focus is. If you are on the lookout for a way to get into TV presenting, your ears prick up when you overhear someone talking about working in TV, or your eyes are drawn by a newspaper article on a famous TV presenter's career and how they started. If you have convinced yourself, however, that TV is too tough to get into, you're more likely to notice stories about how cut-throat TV is. Whatever your belief is about the world, you tend to notice the supporting evidence for that belief.

So, whether or not you choose to believe that the power of quantum physics, the universe or God is helping you out, there is no doubt that getting clear on what you do want and focusing on that will bring you better results than focusing on what you don't want. The question then is how do you create a more optimistic outlook?

Introducing your nemesis

You cannot successfully survive the rollercoaster to transform your life from worker to player unless you master the inner game of play: those unhelpful doubts, beliefs and habits that hold you back. To do that, you will need to tackle your nemesis.

If you can't work out what you want to do with your life, if criticism cuts you to the bone, if you're haunted by negative visions of the future, if you're creatively blocked, if you're a perfectionist or procrastinator, or if your mood takes a dive at the smallest trigger, there's one culprit behind it all.

It's the number one block to playing and it's the enemy of your creativity, happiness and even your wealth. And the enemy is inside you. It's a sub-personality referred to in Gestalt psychology as the 'top dog'.

The top dog is the part of you that says the most damning things:

➡ You can't write to save your life.

➡ So now you want to be a starving artist?

➡ You've always been useless with money.

➡ You're mad to change career in a recession.

➡ If you quit your job, you'll lose your house and end up living in a cardboard box on the street.

And if it doesn't come out as words, you might see images in your mind or feel sensations in the body which represent the same message. When you believe and obey these messages, you limit your playfulness, your creativity, your happiness and your life. Every creativity exercise ever invented was designed to get past your top dog.

Others call top dog the internal critic but I find it more helpful to name it as a separate sub-personality. And the word 'critic' suggests it might give some constructive criticism. The top dog's messages are not constructive. Even if they contain a seed of something true, the shame it comes wrapped in will only demotivate you.

The top dog grew inside you as a child with repeated messages from your parents and other significant authority figures. The same people who taught you important things like "Don't run into the road" and "Keep away from the fire" also taught you less useful ideas like "Don't show off", "You have to sacrifice your happiness to be successful" and "No one enjoys their job". Now these messages are a deeply ingrained habit within your own mind – they are the language of your top dog.

The quality of your life is determined by the quality of your internal dialogue.

Pete Cohen, executive coach, trainer and TV presenter

Origins of the top dog

Babies know what they want and express it freely. Hungry? Just scream. They don't have creative blocks. Of course, this isn't a great way for adults to behave so we raise our children to act in a more sociably acceptable way. But sometimes teaching good behaviour isn't done cleanly. It strays into criticism, shame and humiliation: snapping at the boy who cries, laughing at the girl who gets angry, the silent flick of the eyebrows that disapproves of a child 'showing off'. It's these incidences that create your top dog.

In reality, these messages were fuelled by the fear and anxiety of the person giving them. And that fear and anxiety was learned in *their* childhood. So your top dog is driven by fear – fear of failing, making a fool of yourself, getting hurt or being humiliated.

There's not much logic to it either. It often gives conflicting messages, such as "You should stand up for yourself" and "Don't make yourself unpopular". After all, this is a very young part of you. Have you ever seen two young children walking down the street and the elder sibling is admonishing the younger using their parents' language: "Oh, I don't know what we are going to do with you!" That's all your top dog is doing – aping the messages from your parents.

In a strange way, your top dog is actually trying to protect you – like the person who is self-conscious about their weight and feels compelled to make a joke about it before anyone else does. But the message only serves to make you feel worse.

Top dog messages are culturally influenced. Classic British ones are "Don't get your hopes up", "Don't get ideas above your station",

"Don't show off" and even the shockingly unhealthy "I want never gets". Australia has 'tall poppy syndrome', the idea that if you achieve something that most haven't, you will be resented and attacked for it. America has 'Stay in your lane' to admonish people for daring to comment on anything outside of their core topic.

We hypnotise ourselves through these kinds of habitual thoughts into mistaking unhelpful beliefs for facts of life. We become convinced that 'you can only get rich by doing something you don't enjoy' or that you're 'just not one of those lucky people born with talent'. I meet a lot of people with very different beliefs but the one thing they all have in common is that they see their beliefs as the way the world really is. And this is despite the fact that each client believes such different things. Clients tell me that it's impossible to change career after 30, or after 40, or after 50. And all I can think is "Well, at least one of you is wrong!"

Remember, just because you think something doesn't mean it's true.

Taming your top dog

The greatest mistake we all make is to take the top dog as the voice of reason. It is not. So your first step to managing your top dog for greater creativity and happiness is to identify it. Start today to notice your internal dialogue and if you spot something that might be your top dog, simply label it, "Ah, that sounds like top dog."

This is particularly important when you hit a setback. Know your pattern. What are the kinds of things you find most difficult to deal with? When things didn't go your way in the past, what happened? If you gave up, what was the top dog message at the time that discouraged you? If you managed to get back on the horse, what helped you do it? Did you read a motivating book, speak to a friend or just stop thinking about it for a while? Make a note and remember to use it the next time you hit the down cycle. If you have a friend who always cheers you up, put their number on speed dial now.

Sometimes it's not even a setback that's the trigger. Have you ever suddenly lost motivation on something without knowing why? You start off on some project really excited and a little while later feel completely deflated. Or you find you've simply moved on to something else without even thinking about it. Notice what happened to throw you off track. Was there something you told yourself without even registering it? This is a top dog message.

The next step is to challenge top dog's messages. When you catch a negative message, think of the more supportive alternative. When top dog says, "What's the point in starting? You never finish anything" note it and find the counter argument: "Sure I will. I finished a big project last month that looked impossible and I'll finish this one too." This might sound a little crazy to talk back to yourself, but you're already having an inner dialogue, and you might as well make it a more positive one. If you're struggling to find a positive response, imagine you were advising a friend. What would you say to them in this situation?

If you're not sure if a message you've caught is one you should change – perhaps because it appears to be stating the truth – ask yourself if you would say it in exactly that form to a friend. If not, you shouldn't be saying it to yourself. It's remarkable how we tell ourselves things we would never say to others.

The key is habit. Every time you catch a critical thought and remember to replace it with a supportive one, you build the habit and make it easier to do it again. Not only that, but you will also affect your own brain chemistry. Every time you have a negative thought, chemicals are released in the brain and the rest of the body that make you feel worse. Every time you have a positive thought, chemicals are released that make you feel good.

This is not something you can change overnight but if you could spend just one whole day interrupting every negative thought and introducing its more supportive opposite, you would find that you were strangely happier that day than at any other recent time – without any special reason to be so. And when you make it a habit, you build structures and connections in the brain that make it easier to do again.

Things that help you tame your top dog include psychotherapy, meditation, cognitive behavioural therapy (CBT) and emotional freedom technique (EFT). I've used all of them and in particular I've been in psychotherapy and in a men's group for many years. I've grown from a point in my youth where I had pretty much zero self-esteem and frequent anxiety and depression to a point where I am happy and productive and consider myself to be of above average mental health in some regards.

If you don't want to wait that long to tame your top dog, one of the quickest ways to reinforce your positive internal dialogue is to hang out with supportive people.

Build your support team

Isolation is the dreamkiller.

Barbara Sher, American careers expert and author of five books

What company do you keep? If you want to turn yourself from a worker into a player and escape conventional jobs, you will never do this if the only people you ever spend time with are other people stuck in jobs they don't enjoy. If you're self-employed and struggling to make a living, you will probably never make a good income if all the people you hang out with are struggling too. Why? Because we can't help but take on the opinions, beliefs and habits of the people we spend the most time with. If we're out of step with those around us, what we want will seem abnormal or unusual. Human beings are built to adjust to the people around them. Just remember that you can choose the community you want to fit in with.

When I survey people wanting to do something more creative with their lives, one of their biggest reported challenges is lack of confidence. Whatever it might look like, even the most successful people have to manage their own confidence at times. Here are two important questions I ask clients who are lacking confidence: "What is your top dog telling you?" and "Who do you spend time with?" If your top dog often tells you things that shake your confidence, you can counter this by spending time with positive people who will support you in your projects.

You must create your own support team. Find a small group of four or five people to meet with regularly. Use the group to encourage each other, comfort you when you have a setback, and hold you accountable to do what you say you're going to do.

Do you want to know the secret of getting things done when you're totally undisciplined and a chronic procrastinator? Set a release date as we saw in Secret three and ensure that other people hold you to it. Here's how my friend James did it. He wanted to try creating instrumental music for television but knew he was likely to procrastinate on doing it. So he agreed with his creativity group that he would bring a new finished piece of music to their meeting every fortnight and play it to them. If he didn't, he would pay them a forfeit of £50. It's remarkable what a little external pressure – even self-created – can accomplish. James met all his deadlines, paid no forfeits and ended up creating more music in that period than at any time before.

Stop imagining you're going to wake up one day with great self-discipline. Instead, start building your own support team now. You can start by just finding one other person who you know will be supportive and will take action. Agree to meet them every two to four weeks. Put the appointment in your diary and agree what each of you will have done by then. Show your results when you meet. You'll be amazed how much work you get done the night before your meeting!

Myth 9: People who are successful don't need support (advice, mentoring, coaching, therapy)

The secret to solo success is . . . it's impossible. You can't achieve anything of any great significance on your own. The myth of the lone entrepreneur who did it all on their own is possibly the most dangerous one yet. The fact is people who want to achieve extraordinary things create extraordinary levels of support for themselves: coaches, trainers, advisers, therapists and inspiring peer groups.

A quick word of warning before we move on: be careful who you share your dreams with. Pick supportive people, not the cynical people critical of everything (cynicism is just a way for very fearful people to manage anxiety). Our instincts are usually pretty good on this if we'll only listen to them.

When someone is damning of your new direction, just reflect for a moment on their lives. How is their career going? What's their life like? Do they enjoy it? Or are they miserable and moaning about it all the time? Even if they enjoy their life, would you want it? If you don't want their results, think twice before taking their advice.

Feeling scared yet?

Life shrinks or expands in proportion to one's courage.

Anais Nin

If you're not scared at least some of the time, you're not doing it right. Fear is an inevitable companion when you take the risk to create a different kind of life for yourself. Your ability to manage it is a fundamental factor in how far you can go.

When you start to experience worry, anxiety or naked terror, this is a great time to call on your support team. Get some calming input from someone reliable and ask for some practical steps you can take.

Check what your top dog is saying that's adding to the fear. Fear is something you *do*, not something that happens. Don't believe me? Think of a jumbo jet full of passengers about to take off. Some of them will feel very afraid, some will feel excited, some will feel bored, some will be asleep. Yet they are all on the same plane. What's the difference? The thoughts and images each individual passenger is creating. The fearful passenger is creating visions of the plane crashing, interpreting each sound as a sign of something wrong and telling themselves that planes crash all the time and they are not the lucky type.

Dealing with your fear is one of the most important things you can do. Successful people typically hold an optimistic view of the world and know how to manage what fear they do experience.

Here's a little-known secret: most people think success is determined by how hard you work. While of course there will be times when you have to put an enormous effort in to pull a project off, success is just as often about daring to do a project that scares the hell out of you because you know it will move you forward massively. Say, taking on a well-known client or organisation, volunteering to give your first public talk, hiring your first member of staff, or just getting the hang of going live on social media. There are plenty of people toiling away at the small things that will never get the results they want, when they could put the same effort into something bigger (and scarier) and take a giant leap forward.

When you're doing OK as you are, it's easy to focus on all the possible risks of doing something new. Just remember when you're afraid of taking a risk that there is a risk to *not* doing something. The risk of not changing your career is that you wake up ten years later and find you're still in a job you dislike. The risk of not taking on an exciting new project is that you are giving up all the wonderful things that would have happened in your life had you dared to do it. You need to be willing to give up the good enough to go for the great.

It is when we all play safe that we create a world of utmost insecurity. It is when we all play safe that fatality will lead us to our doom. It is in the 'dark shade of courage' alone that the spell can be broken.

Dag Hammarskjöld, Secretary General of the United Nations, 1962

POWER-UP: Think like an entrepreneur

I want to encourage you to change the way you approach your projects and to start thinking and acting like an entrepreneur. You see, the education system does not teach us how to create change in the world. It teaches us to be passive, wait for instructions, check we have permission, and hunt for the approved correct answer to a problem. That trains us to be a 'workerbot', not a player or entrepreneur.

We have to overturn that training to start thinking for ourselves, try things no one has tried before, and find our own original solutions. It also means a critical shift from being a passenger to a driver.

I see a lot of beginning entrepreneurs set an objective like running an event or selling a service for the first time and say "I'll see if it works". This is the stance of the passive workerbot and will not get you what you want. Make the decision right now to switch from wondering if it will work to declaring "I am going to f**king well make this work". And then throw everything you have at it – as Charlie Thuillier did at the beginning of his Oppo journey to make a healthy ice cream.

How to be unstoppable

It's pretty much inevitable you will get what you really want if you just don't stop. Just remember that if you're flexible, there will be more than one way to have the experience you want even if your original vision doesn't pan out.

The key is that with each play project, you keep fine-tuning your trajectory to move closer and closer to getting paid to play. Use the feedback you're getting, both internal and external, to guide you. External feedback includes your results and the critique of others. Internal feedback is what the experience is like for you. Is it enjoyable or does it look like it will be when you've got the hang of it? Does it feel like you're in flow? This approach of experimentation and course correction is sometimes referred to as 'Ready, Fire, Aim'.

If you launch a play project and find that you're not enjoying it as much as you hoped, that it doesn't feel like the right direction, or you're not getting the results you expected, don't just quit. Think about how you can change the project to make it work better for you. Something attracted you to this in the first place – don't just throw it out. If you set out to become a public speaker but find that conventional after-dinner speaking isn't working for you, think again about what part of the experience originally excited you. How can you feel that in a different way? If it was the thought of inspiring others, you could try teaching or running small work- shops for your next play project. If the experience you wanted was to share your humour, try a stand-up comedy course.

Once you've finished each play project, you'll be in a different place to where you started and your next project can build on this base. By doing this, you can set off without knowing exactly where you're heading and play your way to something that works for you. This is a very different experience from that of people who repeatedly take a few tentative steps in one direction then retreat before shuffling off in a different direction only to return once more to the place where they started.

Life as a player takes plenty of time and effort and it's not going to be 100% fun every day. The whole point is to keep moving on and expanding what you thought you were capable of. This means times of challenge, risk, fear and setbacks.

If you wake up one day and don't feel like doing what you promised someone, you still do it because keeping your promises is an essential part of getting paid to play. If you find you frequently don't feel like doing something, it's time for a change. The good news is that even previously quite boring tasks become more enjoyable when you're doing them for yourself. There's a big difference between having to sweep the floor in some dead-end job and sweeping the floor of the shop you just rented, ready to open it to the public. As entrepreneur and author Derek Sivers puts it, "If you're changing somebody else's baby's diapers that feels like work. But if it's your own kid, that doesn't feel like work."

A fundamental part of the shift from worker to player is to take total responsibility for your own working life. It takes time to stop thinking like a worker and blaming others (or the economy) for your situation. Turn the focus back on yourself and ask again and again what you can do to improve the situation. This is a big shift and can sometimes feel like turning an oil tanker around.

Be willing to have uncomfortable conversations. One of the greatest skills you can learn is to be willing to ask people for what you need. Ask someone to mentor you, to buy your product or service, or ask an employee to redo a piece of work. Sometimes these are not comfortable things to discuss. Most people avoid having uncomfortable conversations – they don't go up to someone famous and ask to talk to them, interview them or work for them. Most people don't cold-call a radio station and ask to be interviewed about their project.

But then most people don't end up with the life they want. If you do what everyone else does, you'll get what everyone else gets.

Dare to have uncomfortable conversations and you'll soon see how your results differ to others. And if it all goes horribly wrong and you slink away cringing at what just happened, just remember that you dared to do something that most don't. You'll laugh about it later. Probably.

Anyone who has never made a mistake has never tried anything new.

Albert Einstein

Stop asking for permission

Are you stuck in the permission trap? Are you waiting for someone to tell you that what you want is possible? Are you spending a lot of time asking and exploring whether you can do what you want to do? Are you researching options and eliminating them one by one? Are you asking: "Is it possible to have a career in X?", "Is it crazy to start a business in Y?" or "Could I ever write a book?"

Stop asking *if* you can have what you want, but ask *how* you can have what you want. When you pose yourself a question, your mind gets to work on answering it even when you're busy doing something else. Ask *whether* you can do something and your mind produces a list of pros and cons. Ask *how* you can do something and your mind comes up with all the ways to do it. Which is going to move you forward? (If after a few days of pondering, the *how* question is still drawing a blank, you can often get unstuck with a *who* question: "Who would know how to do this?" or "Who could put me in touch with the right person to move me forward?")

Stop asking for permission from others to do what you want to do, whatever it may be. If you want it make it happen.

Take some tips from the world's best expert on your success

When you're facing a challenging project, consult the best expert in the world on your success – you. Look back at how you achieved all your life's significant achievements to date: finding your home, making the move, finding your partner, making your relationship work, how you've got a new job or got over a difficult illness. What did you do that made these achievements possible? What worked? How can you use the same strategies now?

When I look back, I realise that pretty much everything I have ever achieved has been due to two factors. First, I started on the project simply because I was interested in it, and second, I finished it because I had an external deadline to share the results that could not be moved. The deadline was the only way to get over my natural perfectionism and procrastination. I made the final decision on my first home and bought it in the two weeks before I quit my job so that I could honestly say I was employed when I signed the mortgage. If I didn't, it might have been very difficult to get a mortgage at all. For every achievement, there was usually a gun to my head, figuratively speaking. I'd love to say this wasn't so but knowing that it is, I can use it to my advantage. Now I know to always agree a release date with other people: a date that I simply have to meet.

Tim Smit is creator of the Eden Project, the remarkable visitor attraction in Cornwall with two giant tropical biomes. He has achieved an enormous amount and yet described himself to me as 'fundamentally lazy' and 'one of the least focused people you could ever meet'. I asked him what drives him to take on these projects rather than just taking it easy. His answer: "The fear of death and a rash desire to make unlikely promises. Which I then have to fulfil or lose face as a consequence."

What works for you? It might be making it fun, or getting loads of support, or getting expert advice. Whatever it is, use it now.

POWER-UP: How to cheat

If you want to accelerate your journey to getting paid to play, try cheating. If someone else has ever successfully done what you're trying to do, chances are you can too. How did they do it? Steal their strategies. Don't steal the content of what they did, steal *how* they did it. How does that writer make such a good living? How did that relatively new band get known so quickly? How did that person get into advertising with so little prior experience? How does that agency win so many projects? How did that software start-up get going without venture capital? Find out, then copy it.

One of the most useful things you can steal is someone's business model. How do they attract attention? What is the first step new clients take to work with them? What do they offer them after that? Where do they make the most money? Perhaps they run low-cost live events and then sell expensive consulting packages or programmes to the attendees. Or they run quirky public projects that win media attention that then attract new corporate projects that are more lucrative. You can do the same.

Myth 10: Famous people are just different from me

Of course, none of this will help you if you're in the habit of thinking of the very famous and successful as a different species. They're human just like you. Sure, talent is a factor but often a lot less than you think. Model their beliefs, thoughts, behaviours and language and you'll be on the way to modelling their success. Be wary of assuming that successful people had some advantage (money, connections, status) that you don't. There will be someone somewhere who had no more advantage than you and still made it. Find them and model them.

Take the Millionaire Test to stay on track

As you play out your journey to doing what you really want to do for a living, check in every day on how it's going and adjust your course accordingly. How do you do this? By using the Millionaire Test.

At the beginning of the day when you first wake up, ask yourself these two questions:

1. If I was already a millionaire, would I choose to do what I am about to do today?

Write down your response.

2. If I had a blank diary today and all the money I could want, what would I *choose* to do with this day?

Write down your response.

If the response is that you would actually take the day off and sit on a beach, then ask how you can achieve some of that experience. Can you actually take the day off? If not, can you find some space to do nothing? If you're nowhere near a beach, can you go swimming after work and then sit by the pool reading a book? Or should you make time to book your next holiday today?

If the Millionaire Test keeps showing that you wouldn't choose to do your work today, it's time to change your work.

You can also use the Millionaire Test throughout the day for the smaller decisions you make. I went to a networking event recently with lots of 'important' people from big companies. I found myself thinking that I should go speak to that guy from the multinational corporation, as he could be an important contact. The problem was I ended up having conversations I wasn't really interested in and realised I was bored. I was choosing people I thought I *should* talk to, not the ones I really wanted to – a habit ingrained from my years of consultancy work in big corporations.

Then I remembered my mantra: If I were already a millionaire, would I do this thing I am considering right now?

I realised that if I was already a millionaire I would just talk to whoever looked interesting to me or who I knew was involved in a project I genuinely wanted to know about. I started to do this that night and met a couple of great people and had fascinating conversations, ones that spurred new ideas and new connections for my business, connections I would *love* to make. One of the people I spoke to went on to speak at an event I ran in London.

Imagine what would happen if we always worked on this basis. We would make natural connections with people we enjoy spending time with. Our projects or businesses would continue to grow with less strain and a lot more fun.

Moment by moment, this simple, rather materialistic-sounding question will guide you towards getting paid to play. On the way it's still important, obviously, to do the things you promised even when you're not in the mood for it. And you might take some projects that are not exactly what you would choose to do but are a good stepping stone to get you to your ultimate ideal.

Of course, you could just ask yourself if you really feel like doing this, but it's amazing how many of my clients cannot answer questions like that effectively – thanks to the influence of the top dog.

If you want to make a habit of using the Millionaire Test, carry around a reminder of it. You may need to change the wording to work for you. 'Millionaire' can mean many things but to my mind implies a level of established wealth that, while not allowing you to retire for good, would give you a great quality of living without working for several years. This is a good position from which to make choices about your work – the heat is off but you may still need to work further down the line.

POWER-UP: How to make progress when you've got no time nor energy

Are you struggling to find the time for your project? Are you creating a new career while still busy working in your old one? There is a way you can still keep making progress: by doing little and often. Carve out micro-blocks of super-focused time to do what is most important to move you forward. Could you spare ten minutes of time at some point in the next 24 hours? You'll be surprised at what you can do in just ten minutes when you're prepared and you focus completely on the task in hand. If you come home exhausted at the end of a day at your current work, you might not feel like doing anything. The fact is that motivation often comes *after* you start something, not before.

Here's how to keep going even when you have very little time to invest. It's a technique I call 'microblocking' and I've taught it to thousands of people on my programmes. Many report that it is a habit that has changed their lives and they continue to use for many years. Microblocking also works brilliantly if you have a task you've been putting off because you have some kind of anxiety or resistance to it. Microblocking is the procrastination-destroyer.

1. Think of the next task you need to do to move your play project forward. What single thing will have the biggest impact for the least amount of time spent – even if you don't get the whole thing finished in one microblock? Write it down.

2. Decide how long your microblock will be: 20 minutes is a good one to start with but it can be as short as ten minutes or as long as 52 minutes (a study by the Draugiem Group found that the most productive people worked for 52 minutes then took a 17-minute break).

3. Write down what you can do in this microblock. Don't go writing things like 'Learn French' or 'Plan business'. Rather write 'Do exercise 10 in French book', 'Search online for three good articles on making money from a podcast and bookmark them to read later' or 'Read the three articles bookmarked yesterday'.

4. Get out your diary and write it in as a real appointment: e.g. 7:00 to 7:20 Do French Exercise 10.

5. Turn up for your appointment. Make this as real a commitment as if you had a doctor's appointment. If something absolutely critical comes up you might move it, but otherwise you stick to it. You never just skip it.

6. Switch off your phone, your email and anything else you don't need that might distract you. Tell others who might interrupt that you are busy.

7. Get a timer that counts down (you can use an app but I quite like an old-fashioned kitchen timer that counts down the minutes and seconds) and set it to 20 minutes or whatever time you've allocated. Place the timer right in front of you and set it counting down. This will help keep you focused.

8. Do exactly what you wrote down that you were going to do.

9. When the timer goes off, you can stop – even if you haven't finished the task. (But if you're now feeling motivated to continue, do.)

10. Before you file your notes, or close your document, decide what you will do in your next microblock. Write it down as your next action so that when you pick up again tomorrow, you know exactly what you're doing. Put your project away where you can pick it up again quickly.

11. Get out your diary and write in the appointment for your next microblock and the action you will take in it.

12. Go and relax!

Of course, for any significant project you're likely to need some big blocks of time to get it done, but until you can free up that time, you will be amazed how much progress you make in your microblocks. And the continual progression will keep your spirits up much more than watching days disappear without doing anything. How many weeks go by with you waiting to spend an hour on your project but never finding the time? Now, can you imagine doing 20 minutes a day, six days a week?

You would be amazed what you can achieve in 20 minutes when you do what's most important and really focus. My client Toby Corballis came up with the great idea to create a podcast called 'Wicked Problems' to raise his profile. I set him the task of getting his first guests but when I checked with him a few weeks later he still hadn't done it. So I told him, "Right, when I next see you I am going to make you sort out your first guests". When we met up I asked for two people he'd love to interview. He named some fascinating academics he'd met while studying and I got him to send them each an email on the spot. He only had his phone with him so he wrote the emails on his phone with some guidance from me on the wording. The two emails took a grand total of 15 minutes to complete. By the time I got home, he texted me to say one of them had replied and agreed to be his first podcast guest. How often are you putting something off because you imagine it will take too long when really you are just procrastinating? Start using microblocking and get it done.

Remember that you don't need to know exactly how you're going to achieve your project. You only need to know the next action and then turn up and do it. Your success is pretty much guaranteed if you do. Just keep moving forward and adjust your course according to your results.

Try doing a microblock first thing in the morning before you start anything else. It's a great way to start your day and ensures nothing can get in the way of doing it. If you can grow the block of time to an hour every day, you can make a huge amount of progress on your project. Be sure to use this technique on Play Wednesday too.

Manage your overwhelm, not your time

It's easy to get overwhelmed these days. We have all too much to do and too much information to manage. Even with the discipline to be ruthless with your tasks and information, the problem will never go away. Your to-do list will not all be ticked off when you die.

Overwhelm is one of your greatest obstacles on the way to getting paid to play. And creative people are particularly prone to it. Why? Because the creative personality does not think in a structured way. We don't have a strong sense of time. We get absorbed in something and hours fly by. It's the ability to forget time altogether that allows us to go so deeply into the creative process. We don't naturally think in a sequential way. We can see everything needed to make a project happen but without any timeframe, so everything looks like it needs to be done right away. The result is overwhelm. Overwhelm feels terrible, so when it happens our response is often to stop altogether. We collapse in a heap or more subtly, we find we've started browsing YouTube or scrolling through Facebook – anything to take our mind off the overwhelm. This is why overwhelm often passes for procrastination or, worse, laziness.

I think of this as an in-built tilt switch. To be a great pinball player, you have to shake the machine around a bit. But if you hit it too hard, the tilt switch activates and the whole machine shuts down. Your job is to notice when your tilt switch has activated, realise it's overwhelm, and do something to address it. The answer is always to break down your task into smaller chunks and focus only on the next chunk you have to do.

Have you found yourself watching TV when you've promised yourself you'd plan your whole website today? Break it down. What's the first thing you have to do? Make it something that lasts no more an hour. How about choosing which five pages you're going to create? Or writing the three main points you want to make on the homepage. Can you do a 20-minute microblock right now?

If you get stuck, call in a friend who finds it easy to plan their time. They'll quickly be able to look at what you have on your plate and tell you the first five things to do and in what order.

Moment by moment you can do simple things to reduce your overwhelm. Have a good diary. Write everything down, don't carry essential information in your head. Leave it free for thinking. Be realistic – write short lists for each day with the three things that are most important to do.

Also check what your top dog is saying about this task that has overwhelmed you. Is it something pessimistic? If it's telling you the project is bound to fail, or you should have done it ages ago, you won't be very motivated to work on it. Is it about perfectionism? Perfectionists are even more prone to overwhelm because their top dog tells them everything they do must be flawless. It's better to finish something that's good than to abandon yet another project because you can't make it perfect. If your perfectionism means you're not putting anything out into the world, dare to make something *good enough* and release it.

How to manage your brilliant ideas

Do you have more ideas than you know what to do with? Resist the temptation of the shiny new idea when you're in the middle of something else. If you pursue everything you think of, you'll never get anything finished. Create a place to keep all your good ideas. When a new one comes to you, store it where you know you'll be able to find it so you can get on with what you were doing.

When you start a whole new project, the very first thing you should do is create a repository for all the ideas you'll have: whether it's a talk you've just been booked to do, a website you're going to build or a product you've decided to make. Start a fresh notebook, or do as I do and start a new entry in Evernote or Apple Notes. Then whenever you have another idea, open the file and jot it down. You might find the first draft of your talk almost writes itself.

When you have a great idea and you know you want to press 'Go' on it, don't hang around.

What you actually do within 24 hours of having a creative idea will spell the difference between success and failure.

Buckminster Fuller, American designer and inventor

Ideas have a half-life. Wait too long before you act on them and there's a chance you'll look back at your notes and wonder what on earth you were talking about. If it looks like the right project for you now to get paid to play, don't waste time getting it launched. "Money likes speed", as author Joe Vitale likes to say.

How to be a creative genius

All children are artists. The problem is how to remain an artist once we grow up.

Pablo Picasso

Learn the tricks to unlock your own creative genius and you'll produce far grander results for a lot less effort. Don't believe the myths about creativity. It's easy to assume great works of art fell out of their creator complete, but in fact they are far more often *sculpted*. Sculptures start as a shapeless block of marble. The sculptor chips away week by week until a rough form starts to emerge. Eventually, the final form is revealed in all its beauty. Any creative process works in a similar, iterative way, but it's easy to forget this and expect we can create something brilliant in one sitting. Here's a much better way.

1. Be clear about what problem you are trying to solve or what outcome you want to achieve. "A problem well defined is half solved", as psychologist John Dewey once said.

2. Work on your project a little every day, ideally first thing in the morning. In between, your subconscious will work on it. Aid it by doing something simple and physical – walking, gardening, washing up.

3. Record your ideas. Creativity researcher Robert Epstein says that those we consider creative may simply have good 'capturing skills': that is, they take all their ideas seriously and record them. So take your playbook and pen everywhere and note anything that comes to you about your project whether it's in bed, on the train or at work. You can even buy a waterproof notepad to capture those great ideas you have in the shower.

4. Think *quantity* not *quality*. "The best way to have a good idea is to have lots of ideas", as chemist and peace activist Linus Pauling once said (and he's one of the few people in the world to have won two Nobel Prizes). Generate as many ideas as possible, write for a set period of time per day, or take a set number of photos per week. This takes the pressure off you getting it 'right' and thereby generates more creative results. Later, go back and choose your best results. Always keep the processes of creating and editing separate as they require different modes of thinking. One is adding to your content, the other is taking it away. Try to do both at the same time and you end up with a brain-freeze.

5. If you get stuck, brainstorm with friends or colleagues and remember that no idea is too wacky in a brainstorm. Or try talking about it to someone for ten minutes while they simply listen. When I was a software developer it was quite common for one of us to get stuck on a technical problem. We'd get up from our seats, walk over to a colleague, start explaining the problem and before we even finish the explanation go "Ah! I know what to do", then walk back to our own desks. Just the

act of talking about the problem out loud had shaken the solution loose from the depths of our own minds.

6. If you're on your own, try writing continuously on the topic without stopping for ten minutes and see what comes out.

When I tried my hand at stand-up comedy, people would ask me how I came up with my material. And I would tell them it's not as difficult as you might think. Carry around a notebook and write everything you can think of that might be funny whenever it occurs to you. Then try the material out on people and edit out the weak stuff. You'll eventually be left with five minutes of good material you can go and perform. World famous comedians still do this. I saw Russell Brand perform in a small bar in London at a weekly event he charged £10 for because he was developing material for an upcoming tour.

The power of 'creative idling'

Idleness for me is not a giving up on life but a spirited grabbing hold of it.

Tom Hodgkinson, editor of The *Idler* and author of *How to be idle*

Idle time is an essential part of the creative process. There will be times you need to put a huge amount of effort into a project. Taking breaks, doing something completely different, spending some time playing with your children, and bunking off for the afternoon can all help you refresh. It's also just a kinder way to treat yourself. If you're going to be your own boss you might as well be a nice one.

Remember to build some time into your schedule for some pure play – the things you love without worrying about turning it into an income. Notice your natural pace and work with it, not against it. Don't try to make yourself into someone else: someone who can work all night, or can focus for four hours straight, or works normal office hours. Work *with* who you are. There is a fashion currently for boasting about how early you get up. 5am? How about 4am? But the fact is a lot of creative people don't do their best work early in the morning so it is pointless to get up early.

Author of *When: The Scientific Secrets of Perfect Timing*, Dan Pink told me in an interview for The Ideas Lab podcast that Benjamin Franklin's adage that "Early to bed, early to rise, makes you healthy, wealthy and wise" simply isn't true for everyone. You need to work out whether you're an owl, a lark or something in-between (what Dan calls a 'third bird') and set your schedule accordingly.

Listen to your body when it's asking for a break. If you don't, you'll find yourself stealing the rest time anyway by losing your attention or getting distracted by something unimportant. You can't cheat your body for very long so you might as well take a real break. You might even get your big breakthrough when you do. JK Rowling was travelling alone on a delayed train from Manchester to London when, as she says, "the idea for Harry Potter simply fell into my head". Over the next four hours "all the details bubbled up in my brain, and this scrawny, black-haired, bespectacled boy who didn't know he was a wizard became more and more real to me".

Physicist Richard Feynman was watching someone messing around throwing a plate in the air in Cornell University's cafeteria when he decided to describe its wobbling movement in equations 'for fun'. The spinning plate equations turned out to be critical to his study of quantum electrodynamics, the work that went on to win the Nobel Prize.

It's necessary to be slightly underemployed if you are to do something significant.

James D Watson, co-discoverer of the structure of DNA

Get a little closer to your natural way of working every day. How close can you get to the way you envisioned living in your year out?

Go on, take a nap

You must sleep sometime between lunch and dinner . . . That's what I always do. Don't think you will be doing less work because you sleep during the day. That's a foolish notion held by people who have no imaginations. You will be able to accomplish more.

Winston Churchill

If you're going to be idle, why not go all the way and take a nap? Naps have been shown in research trials to lower stress hormones and boost productivity and creativity. The effect of a nap is like rebooting your brain and, as Winston Churchill said, "You get two days in one – well, at least one and a half."

If anyone tries to make you feel guilty about napping in the middle of a work day, just remind them that sleep can also be a very productive time. Paul McCartney dreamed the melody for 'Yesterday', and chemist Friedrich August Kekulé discovered the baffling ring shape of the chemical compound benzene after dreaming about a snake biting its own tail. Good napping takes practice. I can now get to sleep in five minutes or less. Use a timer to keep the nap short, around 20 minutes, and you won't wake up groggy.

When you've got the hang of all this, you're in a good place to start angling your play towards something you can get paid for. Read the next Secret to find out how.

Keys to this secret:

→ Dare to hope you can get what you really want and deal with the setbacks when they happen. You guarantee your success if you just don't stop.

→ Identify your top dog and start to tame it.

→ Create your support team and manage your fear.

→ Model other people's successful strategies and your own.

→ Use the Millionaire Test to stay on track.

→ Do little and often if you're short of time and manage your overwhelm.

→ Use the creative genius process and creative idling to maximise your effectiveness.

What you should have now:

→ a strategy to manage yourself to get you where you want to go.

Take ten minutes to play:

→ Try putting one of the strategies in this Secret into action now.

→ Call one person who could be the start of your support team.

Exclusive extras on fworkletsplay.com:

→ Interviews with creative entrepreneurs explaining how they manage their time and their mindset.

→ The secret of good napping.

→ Episodes of The Ideas Lab podcast with Dan Pink on what time you should wake up and Nir Eyal (author of *Indistractible*) on how to control your attention and choose your life.

Secret five
How to play for profit . . . and purpose

An entrepreneur is someone who solves problems at a profit.

T Harv Eker, American entrepreneur, author and speaker

We've now seen how to launch your first play project and manage yourself to keep going when things get tricky. This Secret will show you how to tune your projects towards something people might actually pay you for.

To kick us off, here's a story of a British entrepreneur who was simply following an interest in psychology when he had an idea that could solve a significant problem for millions of people.

Turning a passion into a #1 app

Eight years ago, David Crane was a frustrated web entrepreneur. Whilst often ahead of the game when it came to technology (he founded his first internet business in 1995), none of his ideas had really got off the ground. The latest, a website that allowed people to easily compare the pros and cons of contentious issues, had been folded into a large US charity but he found working for someone else didn't suit him.

He took a few months off to mull over options and this happily coincided with the London Olympics, leading to a fascination with the way athletes' mindset affected their performance. Decades of personal development work had given him a love of behaviour change; maybe now was the time to make this a career. He decided he would become a sports psychologist.

As Dave puts it, "I thought maybe I could help my beloved Arsenal win titles again – there was a team that needed some psychology!"

So he put his spare room on AirBnB, picked up some web development projects to work on part time to keep the money coming in and started a masters degree at the ripe old age of 48.

When it came time for his dissertation he needed an idea.

I had just given up smoking and I noticed that there were no good stop smoking apps. So I thought why don't I create one? There was actually a lot of research literature about what works to change habits like smoking and it wasn't being used in an app. I could combine my love of technology with my love of psychology to learn more about what helps people quit.

It took me and a friend approximately four months to create the MVP [Minimum Viable Product that people could use effectively]. My aim was purely to use the app to gather useful information for research. I wasn't thinking of a business then.

The main feature was a series of 'missions', small quit smoking tasks undertaken daily. Inspiration came from training for my first marathon. I went from a complete non-runner to running four hours non-stop in six months because I had a step-by-step plan and could see the plan working.

I used the same philosophy in the app. I created a stop smoking plan that would get people through the difficult first month and would help them see the progress they're making. The hardest part about behaviour change is keeping going. We need to feel the effort we're making to continually resist cravings is worthwhile so I made sure they could see themselves making progress.

I reckoned I could get 500 people to use the app which would provide good data for my research. When I told my supervisor that he laughed at me – that was a crazy number for a trial at this level.

In reality the app did far better – it started at 300 downloads a week then grew to 2,000. I ended up with 28,000 participants for my research. And the app reviews were great too. It became obvious this could be a real business.

Today, it's Dr Dave. He got his PhD in app-delivered behaviour change, and Smoke Free is the #1 stop smoking app, the most popular and most effective stop smoking app in the world. It's had over 4 million downloads and 135,000 five star reviews and its effectiveness has been proven in two randomised trials with 90,000 participants.

David's company now has two full-time staff, three remote developers and 21 part-time stop smoking experts.

Since I stopped doing what I thought I should do and started doing what I wanted to do, things have really fallen into place. Sometimes working for others, I've felt slightly resentful but with the app and being my own boss, I want to work on it. Doing something I like and am good at keeps me going when things get tough and makes it much easier to resist the pull of the sofa.

Find out more about David's app at smokefreeapp.com

David turned a passion into a business because he could see a chance to solve a compelling need while using the technical skills he already had. So how can you do this? How can you find a way to turn the things you really enjoy doing into something people will pay for? This is where we get into the nitty-gritty of making money. It's time to start thinking like an entrepreneur. Are you ready to discover the magic key to getting paid for playing? Here it is: Solve a problem.

If you want to turn your playing into profit, the key is to do the things you love doing in ways that solve problems for people. Problems are powerful things. Find a good problem to solve and you can bet there'll be a way to make money out of it. Solving people's problems happens to feel good too.

Understanding the power of problems will have a transformational effect on your ability to get paid to play. Here's why. Think about why people spend money. It's predominantly for one of only two reasons: we either want to avoid some pain or experience some pleasure. And out of the two, pain is the far more powerful driver. The pain could be physical (like back pain), emotional (loneliness, unhappiness, boredom), financial (can't afford the next mortgage payment) or even spiritual (feeling unfulfilled).

Whether the pain is mild like feeling bored or something more acute like a toothache, it points to a problem that someone is motivated to pay to solve. Think of home insurance – we buy it not because it feels great to be insured but because we feel anxious not to be. Worrying about losing all your belongings if you got burgled is a problem, and it's one that most of us are willing to spend money to solve.

In fact, you could argue that even luxury purchases are influenced by the desire to change an unsatisfactory situation. How many holidays in the Northern hemisphere are booked in the depths of January when the climate is at its darkest and coldest?

People creating their own income for the first time often miss the importance of solving problems. They make the mistake of offering services that are a 'nice to have' not a 'must-have'. If you do this, you'll find it much more difficult to make a living. We've all seen the inventor peddling some contraption that's terribly clever but that no one really needs, or the new freelancer offering some service that sounds very nice but no one ever buys. The problem is that something will always be more important than buying what you're offering. People today are busy. We all have long 'to do' lists and overflowing email inboxes. That can be either good news or bad news for you. Make sure you offer something that's already on people's to-do lists and it's good news.

David knew that lots of people had tried to stop smoking but lapsed (including himself). The problem was sticking with the habit of being 'smoke free' and that's a problem that featured prominently on people's list of concerns to do something about.

When somebody knows they have a problem, you don't have to convince them they need a solution – they already want one. You only need to show them that you are capable of providing that solution and that it's worth the price you're asking. Don't waste your time offering things you have to persuade people they need in the first place. It can be done, but it's very hard work and you may end up broke before you succeed.

Let's go problem-hunting

Look at the project you've chosen to play with. Hopefully you've based it on something you think you will enjoy doing and you also have some talent or expertise for. The question now is what problem could this project solve for people? For our purposes a problem is simply a situation a person or organisation is in that they are dissatisfied with – because that's something they're motivated to solve.

Here are some examples of how to identify the problem you solve while doing what you love.

Enjoy building attractive little websites? You could solve the common problem of people feeling overwhelmed by all the options and expenses of building a website by offering website design with a set number of simple customisable designs.

Want to consult to organisations to make them better places to work? Srabani Sen joined my Pioneer Programme to help organisations improve their diversity and inclusion. Her market research showed that some traditional diversity and inclusion businesses not only left people feeling judged, the solutions they offered didn't help shift the behaviours that were blocking progress and so failed to achieve long-lasting change. Her experience as a charity CEO meant that she knew for change to happen, the journey has to be fun, engaging and feel psychologically safe, something that was lacking in many traditional diversity and inclusion services. Srabani created Full Colour to solve this problem. She has now consulted to well-known organisations, is regularly invited to speak at events, and has become a columnist for Charity Times magazine.

Enjoy sorting out other people's messy lives? Thinking of becoming a virtual assistant? What problem would you find interesting to help with? People overwhelmed by the complexity of organising events? People who are driven to distraction by their admin tasks interrupting their creative projects? Small businesses that never find the time to dedicate to marketing even though they need more sales?

Passionate about practising complementary therapies? You could specialise in a specific problem area such as helping pregnant women who commonly suffer fatigue, stress and back pain.

Love creating art? Think art doesn't solve a problem? Artist Jay Versluis created a gorgeous abstract photograph called 'Stripes'. An interior designer saw his photo and realised it solved a problem for a new minimalist office development she was working on. The office was crying out for a striking piece of art to offset the stark simplicity of the building. Jay created a back-lit installation of the piece measuring a huge 12 feet by 12 feet and ended up making over £5,000.

Invented a quirky gadget that might make a good corporate gift? Lots of companies, both big and small, fear being seen as unimaginative or old-fashioned. This problem means they have to keep finding ways to be different and original in everything they do, including the corporate gifts they give away at exhibitions and events. The problem of being seen as just the same as everyone else should not be underestimated – and of course it's one that individuals have too.

Having fun creating a website of humorous writing, images, or video? Even this can solve a real problem – the problem of being bored at work, wanting to escape for a few moments and have a laugh. If the humour is narrowly focused on an obscure hobby or interest, it can also address the isolation people might otherwise feel and provide a sense of community. (For a nice example, take a look at xkcd.com, a geeky webcomic about mathematics and life.)

Think about your current play project. What problem could this solve for people? When you're looking for a problem to solve, look for the emotional language used by the people you're trying to help. They use words like "I'm sick of ", "I'm bored with" or "I'm worried about". When you hear this language, you've found a problem.

Finding the problem

Sophie Boss runs her business Beyond Chocolate with her sister Audrey helping women to stop dieting and overeating and finally enjoy food without guilt, and lose weight. When they first launched, their strapline was 'Transform Your Relationship With Food'. Sophie later attended a marketing workshop and as she explains:

The woman leading it looked at me and said "You know, I don't think anybody wakes up in the morning thinking 'I really must transform my relationship with food'" And she was right. What they do is they think they've got to lose weight or they've just got to stop the dieting madness or they can't do it anymore. And so we decided to change our wording.

The strapline of the book we wrote afterwards is 'Stop yoyo dieting and lose weight for good'. It felt like we were making a big compromise because even though women do lose weight with

Beyond Chocolate, we didn't feel that was the focus of our work. We were keen to explain how Beyond Chocolate was different and how it could help them. What I've discovered is that people are interested in what they want, and they don't necessarily want to know how we do it. Transforming their relationship with food is the 'how', their goal was to end the misery of yo-yo dieting and finally lose weight.

Read more about Beyond Chocolate at beyondchocolate.co.uk

It's easy when you feel strongly about something to try to force a solution on people just because you think it would be good for them. But people don't buy based on your feelings – they buy based on theirs. Identify what they see as the problem and what they want as a solution. Then map what you do accordingly. Sometimes that means you have to sell what they want and then deliver what they need.

POWER-UP: Get specific to get traction

If you've already tried offering your skills and expertise but been dissatisfied with the take-up, stop having broad and generalised discussions about what you can do and instead tune into the people you're trying to help, as Sophie did. Find a specific problem you can address and focus on that.

Here's a very powerful way for you to identify the problem you could solve. Think about the moment that someone finally buys your product or calls you up and hires you. What is happening to them at that exact moment? They may have been thinking about buying your product or booking some of your time for a while but something precipitates them to finally take the plunge. Do you know what it is? I get the most book sales and enquiries about my courses on a Monday when people go back to work after the weekend and are faced with just how unhappy they are in their job. (Those that really hate their work contact me Sunday night when just the thought of going back to work is too much.) And I've put this knowledge to good use. I get a good response when I email people on a Monday morning with a headline that asks, "Can't face another week at work?"

Now let's find the problem that you can solve for people. We're looking for that sweet spot where the things you love doing, and have some real strengths in, can be used to help people with something that's bugging them. It's time for some serious brainstorming.

Write a big list of problems or situations people are dissatisfied with that you reckon you could help with. You don't need to have the complete solution to a problem, but just be able to make some impact on it.

Ask yourself these questions to get you thinking and write down your answers in your playbook:

➡ Look at the play project you defined in Secret three and ask yourself what problem this could solve for other people. What problem could you solve if you changed the focus a little?

➡ Is there a specific industry, niche or group of people you think you'd enjoy working with? If so, what kind of problems do they talk about having? What's the biggest headache in that field right now?

➡ Look back at your moments of magic. What problem (big or small) were you helping people with at that moment?

➡ Within your own life, what problems consistently irritate you that you are well positioned to help with and you might enjoy working on?

→ If you've already got an idea for a business, write down the most important problems this business could solve for your clients or customers.

→ If you're already self-employed, what pressing problems do your clients have that you know you could help with? Think of the services or products you already offer and write down the problems that they solve for your clients.

→ If you currently consult to other businesses (or would like to), what are the pressing problems they have that you can help with? What is going on at the moment people pick up the phone to hire you? You can bet it's a pressing problem. (When I was an independent consultant in broadcast technology, finally realising the problem I solved for clients made it much easier to know exactly where to look for work. For me it was large consultancies winning projects that they have no specific expertise in and so need to quickly hire a subject matter expert like I was at the time.)

→ If you're selling yourself to large organisations, what problem does the person have who is hiring you? You may want to run a workshop to improve staff morale but you must discover what problem their manager sees: perhaps a decrease in performance or high staff turnover.

→ If there are already other providers or solutions in the area you're targeting (and there usually are), what are the problems with their product or service that you could address?

→ Think of your favourite projects that you have done before. What problem did they solve?

→ If your aim is to create a better job for yourself (more on this later), what problem is big enough inside the organisation that people would be willing to hire you to work on?

→ And always check: Is this a problem someone has right now? Are they aware of it? Does it feature on their to-do list?

➡ Start to notice successful businesses you admire and ask yourself what problems they solve. You might not see that they are solving a problem at first but think it through. What problems, for example, does Facebook address that makes 2.5 billion people around the world want to use it?

The mistake many people make when first introduced to this way of thinking is that they describe what the person wants, not what their current problem is. If you enjoy helping people make more money, 'wanting to be rich' is not the problem, nor is 'not being rich'. The problem is something more like 'being fed up with working long hours just to make ends meet and still having to go without a decent holiday'. What we're looking for is the pain or discomfort that people are experiencing *right now*. Picture their life as it is *now* to discover the problem.

Some people think talking about problems like this is being too negative or even manipulative. In fact it is more empathic – it is speaking the language of your customers or followers instead of talking from your perspective all the time. If, for example, I constantly feel under the weather, you will have much more impact on me if you talk about the experience of being fed up with a never-ending series of colds and viruses than if you talk to me about how wonderful it is to be in perfect health. It's difficult for me relate to the ideal end-result right now. Once you have my attention, then you can start to convince me how you could help me have much better health.

If you struggle to think in terms of the negative state your customers are in, and naturally think in positive terms of what they want, try asking yourself these two questions: What is the thing your customers really want in their lives that you can help them get? Now what is it that's currently stopping them from getting it? It's this obstacle that is the real problem you're solving. For example, if you're a personal trainer, your clients want to be fit, healthy and look good. The obstacle (and therefore the problem you solve) is the fact that they don't have the self-discipline or the expertise to easily get fit on their own. Whatever your work is, write down your clients' desire and the obstacle that stops them achieving it without you. You'll find you have far better results when you talk with prospective clients not just about their desires but about this obstacle that stops them getting it.

POWER-UP: Quickly discover what people really want

Knowing the pressing problems of your target market is a hugely valuable thing. If you don't know what they are, ask them. Run some informal market research. This is surprisingly simple and effective. Don't create elaborate surveys and hope strangers will fill them in. Just ask people human to human.

If you're selling to individuals and you already have an email list, send all your contacts an email asking the question "What's your single biggest challenge right now with clutter/losing weight/winning more business (or whatever your area of interest is)?" Thank everybody who replies. The resulting information is priceless. You now know exactly what troubles the people you want to work with most and can set about creating something to help. If you don't have an email list you could ask friends or contacts on social media (but bear in mind this works much better with people you have already built some kind of relationship with).

If you're selling to organisations, it may be better to arrange to meet a few of them on the understanding that you are doing research and ask them "What is the biggest single challenge you face in your industry right now?" Again, not only do you get some fantastically useful information but also this non-salesy approach often has a very nice side-effect that someone might ask if you can you actually help them with it now.

> Few people ever do this but when you stop guessing what people want and actually find out you can create something people will be extremely keen to buy. Speak to ten people and you will have so much more clarity than most people ever will. (And just imagine where you'd be if you spoke to 100.)

Want to change the world?

Are you fed up doing work you don't really care about? Are you looking for something more meaningful? Perhaps you already know there is some part of the world you want to have a positive impact on. If so, make it manageable by choosing a specific problem to solve first. This might be a practical problem: restaurants being unfriendly to children, the high-profile failure of public construction projects to come in on time and on budget, technology being far too complicated to use for elderly users, or the shocking diet of schoolchildren at school and at home.

It might be a global problem: the contribution of inefficient home heating to global warming, the lack of HIV and Aids education in some of the poorest parts of the world, or the lack of understanding between different faiths.

Or you might be drawn to helping people with one of the universal challenges of the human condition: loss, illness, relationship problems, low self-esteem, depression. Often the thing we feel most strongly about is something we have experienced ourselves in some form. Think of ex-smoker David Crane helping others to stop smoking with his app.

Sometimes those challenges that marked our earliest lives leave the biggest impact. Some of us endured poverty, survived illness, suffered an early loss, or were criticised or discouraged by those most important to us. What challenges have you struggled with in your life? The problem you choose to work on might be informed by this experience.

Which problem to solve?

Hopefully you've identified a number of problems you could help solve for people. How do you choose? Here are five questions to help you decide:

1. Can I address this problem while doing something that I really enjoy and I'm good at? If you're just starting out on the journey to get paid to play, this question is the most important one right now. Choose something fun to do.

2. Do I have something I bring that can impact this problem? What talents, skills and knowledge do I already have that will be valuable? If all you have is the idea it will be difficult to make it work.

3. Is this a big enough problem for people? Generally speaking, the bigger the problem and the bigger the impact you can have on it, the more you can get paid for helping with it. Is it the kind of problem people will pay to solve? (If not, it may still be possible to make it work by attracting enough people and charging for advertising or selling other services, but this is often a much longer journey.)

4. Are there plenty of people who have this problem right now? Do I know the kind of people who have this problem? Are they reachable? This is particularly important if you want to solve a relatively mild problem like boredom. You might need to solve it for a lot of people to make it pay.

5. Is it something I care about addressing? If you feel strongly about helping people who have this problem, that's all the better. Is there a problem on your list that you look at and you really want to do something about it, then that's a yes – as long as the other criteria are also met.

Make some notes in your playbook about the problems you will help solve but remember that it's likely to take some time and some investigation to really nail this. Keep coming back to this and clarifying over it over the next few weeks and months.

Once you know what you're going to do for people, all you need to do is find 'em and tell 'em. The next Secret will help do you this by showing you how to play the fame game.

Put it into play

Keys to this secret:

➡ The secret to playing for profit is to solve a problem.

➡ If you don't know what problem to solve, ask the people you work with (or intend to work with) what their biggest problems, concerns and frustrations are.

➡ If you want to change the world, choose a specific problem to address.

What you should have now:

➡ A shortlist of problems you can solve and a favourite one to start with or to investigate further.

Take ten minutes to play:

➡ Think of someone who has the problem you want to help solve. Call them up and arrange to talk to them about it. Find out exactly what the problem is and what kind of solution they would like. Don't try to sell them anything.

➡ Try writing out a description of the problem which you could later use in a social media post to get input from people or on a sales page describing what you do for people.

Exclusive extras on fworkletsplay.com:

➡ Listen to an audio recording that goes deeper into the topic of identifying problems to solve.

➡ Listen to a talk by Sophie Boss from the early days of her business Beyond Chocolate, on its creation and development and an interview with Srabani Sen on how she created her business Full Colour.

➡ Find out about the free 5-Day Business Startup Challenge I run to help people find the problem that they can build a thriving business around.

Secret six
How to play the fame game and win

I am successful because I was willing to give up being anonymous.

Sophia Loren, actress

You should now have some idea of how you can do something that feels like play to you while also providing something people need. All you have to do now is get the message out to those people. And to do that you need to become famous, or at least known, for something. Whether you long to become a household name or simply be respected in your field and win more opportunities, you can play the game your way to create the fame you want. This Secret will show you what to say, who to say it to, and where, when and how to say it.

And you'll be amazed at just what you can become famous for today.

Anything is possible now, you guys

In 2011, New York-born Josh Ostrovsky branded himself 'The Fat Jew' and started posting outrageous memes and videos on Instagram. As *The New York Times* describes it he "parlayed a profane sense of humor that mocks the tropes of social-media culture and the hipsters who propagate them; an apparent affection for pot, pets and grandparents; and his own slovenly, outlandish physical appearance . . . into a huge web following."

Whether it's mocking the attempts of Hollywood celebrities to be cool, doing photo shoots in a thong made from beef jerky and his hair styled in a vertical ponytail, or turning up to interviews wearing a onesie with the zip undone to his belly button, he knows how to use his own outrageous personal brand to draw attention.

The result is 11 million followers on Instagram and *Time magazine* naming him one of the 30 most influential people on the internet.

Josh has had his fair share of criticism. He's been banned from Instagram three times and in 2015 he was accused of posting screenshots of other comedians' jokes on Instagram and Twitter without permission and with the credits cropped out. Josh edited his past posts to credit the authors of the jokes.

He admitted in a 2015 interview with the *Financial Times* that it's still difficult to explain to 'proper adults' what he does.

Not getting all high and mighty about it but it's more like performance art than comedy . . . I won't ever open a soup kitchen but what I do is the next best thing. Pictures are what I can give back to the world. A lot of people have steady careers, health insurance, a pay cheque at the end of the month, a wife and three kids. But that kind of life can get boring. Sometimes you need to see a fat guy sitting in a giant bowl of chilli . . . So if I can make your day a little less shitty, help you 0.001 per cent while your life is falling apart, that feels like a noble undertaking to me.

Aside from being paid for product placement and promotions by global brands, he is also co-founder of Swish Beverages selling wines with irreverent names like White Girl Rose and Family Time Is Hard and more recently a line of canned wines called Babe.

In June 2019, it was announced that Anheuser-Busch had acquired Swish Beverages. This was the brewer's largest wine investment ever, driven by a search for growth as consumers turn away from bland beer brands like Budweiser and Bud Light.

As Josh wrote on his Instagram profile the week the sale was announced, "I sold my wine company to the largest alcohol conglomerate in the world while wearing ass-less leather chaps and having one of the stupidest haircuts of all time. Anything is possible in 2019 you guys. No, but seriously, ANYTHING."

Follow the Fat Jew on Instagram at @TheFatJewish

Whatever your vision of fame, your journey to get there is likely to take a while but you can launch it today. The rules have changed – you no longer have to create the perfect finished product before you start to share your work with the world. The internet has changed everything. Now you can play out your ideas in public on a global stage. You can open up the process and share the output of your project as you work on it. You can invite anyone in the world to contribute to it. Play it out as a work in progress, build a tribe of followers, get valuable input, and explore ways to make money from it. Embrace 'Life in perpetual beta' as American film-maker Melissa Pierce calls it in her documentary of the same name.

Even big companies like Google release everything as 'beta' and implement improvements on the fly. Leading trend firm, Trendwatching, calls this 'foreverism': consumers and businesses embracing conversations, lifestyles and products that are never 'done'.

This is good news for you because when you're just starting out you don't know what your project or business really is yet. Play it out, explore, experiment. Find your unique voice, discover your brand. Invite feedback and ideas on social media. You could even co-create your product or business with the audience it as aimed at. Whatever you do, as soon as your idea is exposed to the air, it will change. It must change as you discover what others see as the real value in your idea.

Want to start a movement? Share your vision and build a following online. Highlight the people and ideas who are aligned with your values. Want to run an event? List your first as a freebie on meetup.com or as a Facebook event. Want to share your expertise? Answer questions on Quora, join Facebook groups and help people out, share your knowledge on Twitter in bite-size portions every day. Offer to answer people's questions and compile your answers for publication as a book or digital download later.

What was once a one-sided conversation from business to customer or star to fan is now a two-way discussion.

deadmau5 shows the power of playing in public

Multi-award-winning music producer, Joel Zimmerman, better known as deadmau5, often livestreams his extended studio sessions as he develops songs. A few years ago he jammed, mixed, and produced for 24 hours straight to develop a song called 'The Veldt', while fans all over the world watched live. He also uploaded each new version of the track to SoundCloud for fans to download and add to.

During his creative process, he announced that he needed to start thinking about the vocal track for the song. Up-and-coming music producer Chris James had been watching deadmau5's stream and set about writing his own lyrics (based on the Ray Bradbury short story) and laying his vocals on top of deadmau5's work. He uploaded his version to SoundCloud for others to hear. What happened next was remarkable.

deadmau5's twitter followers started tweeting him to tell him about Chris's amazing vocal version of his song. deadmau5 decided to check out Chris's work for himself, and here was his response: "Some guy on twitter said he did vocals for this track already. Should I check them out or not? Okay I'll go look. F**k it."

Upon listening to Chris' track, deadmau5 throws his hands in the air in amazement and declares: "Holy sh*t! I am f**king impressed right here!"

Within hours, Chris was on the phone to deadmau5 and his agents to seal a deal. Chris's vocals ended up on a Grammy-nominated musician's song that was named by *Rolling Stone* as one of the 50 best tracks of 2012.

Sharing your creative process in public might feel unfamiliar and uncomfortable for you – whether you're a relatively unknown musician like Chris or a celebrity DJ like deadmau5 – but if you can dare to share more of yourself and your work in process, the benefits are huge. You make connections, build an audience and attract your own luck.

Find Deadmau5 on Twitter, Instagram and YouTube

Real pioneers in any field get there not just by studying but by experimenting and playing. Would you like to be recognised as a pioneer, a thought leader, a true original? Want to do something more than just rehash other people's ideas? Then make your life a laboratory. Test out new ways of doing things and notice what happens. What have you discovered to be true for you? What received wisdom have you found to be a load of nonsense for you? Record it all as lab notes in your playbook. Take the problem you chose to help people with in the last Secret, throw out the rulebook, follow your hunches, and experiment with new ways of solving it. Report what you find and invite others to join the conversation. If you can come up with a new solution, this can be a speedy route to fame.

The Love Challenge

In 2018 I found myself to be single and I recognised that although I've been successful in several areas of life and had some good relationships, I had never enjoyed the dating process. I decided to make it my mission to get the hang of dating. I started to talk about this topic openly on Facebook and found it attracted a huge amount of interest.

I decided I would interview the best experts in flirting, dating and relationships and share what I learned. This quickly attracted the attention of the editor of *Psychologies* magazine, Suzy Walker and she suggested we livestream the interviews to *Psychologies'* 1.3 million Facebook followers and edit the highlights into a podcast. The podcast culminated in me asking for volunteers to go on a date with me and agree to have the evening recorded. It was great fun and a huge learning experience. I then took everything I'd learned and created an online course called 'The Love Challenge' which ended up being one of my highest rated courses of all time and literally changed the lives of many of the participants.

Read more about The Love Challenge at www.thelovechallenge.info

---

You don't have to bare your soul to attract attention (as I did in The Love Challenge) but I do want to encourage you to be more open about your journey. If you think you should keep your business secret read this next myth.

Myth 11: I must keep my good idea secret or someone will steal it

Are you afraid to tell anyone the idea for your project or business in case someone steals it? Ideas are a lot less precious than you might imagine. There are very few totally original ideas: mostly they are just variations on a familiar format. Besides this, it's the execution that really matters. Remember the reality TV show *Big Brother*? If someone described it to you it wouldn't sound that exciting: 'We take a bunch of ordinary unknown people, put them in a house together and video everything they do for a couple of months." It doesn't sound like something that became a prime-time hit in over

60 countries. That's because it's how it's actually executed that matters. The way you execute your idea will be uniquely yours. Someone else with a seemingly identical idea wouldn't produce the same final product because they don't, in reality, have exactly the same vision and approach.

The bottom line is that if you have great ideas, and the worst happens and someone steals your idea, you'll have more of them. The big problem with keeping your idea secret is that you lose the benefit of everyone else who could help you. I often meet people who say they can't tell me their business idea and it's frustrating because I would have been happy to give them a few minutes of free guidance right there and then.

Just use common sense. If all you have is the idea right now and you don't have anything that ties the idea to you (e.g. the right contacts, industry knowledge or specialist skills to make it happen), then use caution when talking with others who have more ability to execute it. However, if you don't bring any strengths or competitive advantages to the idea you should consider whether it is even the right idea for you.

So are you ready to start playing the fame game? Here are the five steps to launch (or relaunch) yourself on to the world. Make it one of your play projects to implement these steps. If you are currently looking for employment rather than starting your own business, these strategies are still very relevant. In fact, following them may allow you to side-step the whole, very limited, world of conventional recruitment and get noticed by someone who can help you create your ideal job. (More on this in Secret nine.)

Step one: Pimp your project

If you want to get known in the new crowded and noisy global marketplace, you have to dare to stand up and stand out. Find a way to juice things up. Don't become a fake, but a larger and louder version of yourself. We're all different, we're all privately a bit quirky or mad or at least obsessed with something others don't care about. Instead of hiding it as the corporate world teaches us to do, use it. If you're a young and hip financial advisor, you could brand yourself as the alternative finance guy. If you're a calm voice of reason in a line of business where everyone sports designer jeans and an edgy haircut, get a pin-striped suit. Whichever it is, dare to be a maverick and break the accepted conventions of your field.

Colour outside the lines. Don't blend in, find a shocking or funny way to name or present your play project (or your whole business) and you'll attract attention without paying for it. Make it news-worthy, find the angle in what you do that makes it interesting, original or entertaining. The more remarkable you are (even if it's simply going to extraordinary lengths to make clients or customers happy), the less hard slog you have to put in to get yourself known.

Marketing is a tax you pay for being unremarkable.

Robert Stephens, founder of tech support company Geek Squad

Sophie Boss on the chocolate effect

We called our business Beyond Chocolate because it was about not worrying about chocolate, beyond making it the enemy or this amazing thing that you shouldn't really have and should think of only from afar. But we could have called it Beyond Peanuts, Beyond Crisps, Beyond Mashed Potatoes, Beyond Anything. The point was to have a name that wasn't scary and that was media-attractive. The fact that we had chocolate in the name of our business meant that the media came to us rather than us having to chase them. We eventually ended up being featured in The Daily Mail, The Independent on Sunday *and* The Observer.

If you're funny, use it. Humour can be a great tool to engage and charm people. When Elon Musk got frustrated with Californian traffic, he decided to form a company to create underground motorways. He called it The Boring Company.

Then he had an idea to raise some fast funds for the company. They created 20,000 flamethrowers with the Boring Company written on them and priced them at $500 a piece.

When the pre-order page went live on the website he tweeted to point out how useful they would be in the event of a zombie apocalypse: "Works against hordes of the undead or your money back!"

But before long he hit a snag as he reported on twitter, "Apparently, some customs agencies are saying they won't allow shipment of anything called a 'Flamethrower'. To solve this, we are renaming it 'Not a Flamethrower'." Within a week he'd sold out, making $10 million for the Boring Company.

Show your personality because people buy people, not just your services or products. Say what you really think. If you hate something that's common in your field, say so. Others will agree and will feel drawn to you as a result. Even those that don't will be tempted to respond (and the algorithms love debate).

I work with many people first striking out on their own. And I am constantly amazed that when they launch their website or brochure, they take everything that makes them different, special, interesting, and talented and strip it out of their marketing. As a result, they end up with a website that looks exactly the same as everyone else's. This is not doing anyone a favour. How can a visitor to your site now tell whether they click with your personality and approach? Think of what's most striking about you – your friendliness, your cheeky sense of humour, your brilliant ideas, your obsession with detail – and build your entire brand around that. Show it in the text and styling of your marketing materials.

In this age, what's different about you, what's unusual about you is your greatest asset. Flaunt your quirks. Use your life experiences. We've all suffered setbacks, challenges and tragedies in our lives and often these are the events that have taught us the most. Use what you've learned.

All the marketing in the world won't help you unless you're doing good work. Live it and breathe it until you become great at it. You can only do that if you've chosen work you love. Build everything around your moment of magic and what is in flow for you and you'll attract people by word of mouth. Your marketing can then amplify the effect by bringing your story to new audiences. Communicate your passion for your work but even more importantly, channel that passion into creating something great that people really love.

When you get this right, you'll find you start to get lucky. As long as you're out there doing the right work, and sharing your journey, you'll find you stumble across the right people and opportunities to help you move to the next stage. This is what I call 'engineering chance'. As long as you have your eyes open, you can take advantage of it.

> *When your energy is right, people and opportunities are attracted to you. When they show up, bill 'em.*
>
> **Stuart Wilde, author of 20 books**

A lot of people have negative associations with marketing, thinking it's about being disingenuous and conning people. It doesn't have to be. For people to enter any kind of relationship with you, whether personal or business, they need to know, like and trust you. Good marketing helps to make this happen more easily. And marketing can actually can be a force for good in itself. At its best, as one of the greatest marketers in the world, Seth Godin says, "Marketing is the generous act of helping others become who they seek to become."

One very useful tool for marketing your work is to be able to tell a good story about it. If you have a compelling backstory to why you started the business, this can often attract more media attention than the content of your business. Harry and Charlie Thuillier for instance got a lot of interest in the early days of Oppo for the fact that they were two young brothers starting a business together.

You can even bring a project proposal to life by treating it like a dramatic story as David Pearl did.

The power of a great story

David Pearl has been singing opera since he was a young boy. After completing his education, he worked as a copywriter during the day and as an operatic tenor in the evenings.

Later he co-founded Opera Circus to meld opera, circus and theatre together and created some award-winning shows. He thought he'd always belong in the world of art but an unexpected call from one of the largest professional services companies in the world drew him into the business world. The company asked for David's help because they wanted to bring the arts into the way they made relationships, solved problems and did business.

David told me the story of what happened next on The Ideas Lab podcast:

> *I sat in their boardroom as they explained what they wanted help with. At the end I asked what their budget was and they said: "The budget is of no consequence. What's important is the quality of your ideas."*
>
> *And I thought I know what you guys are doing, you're trying to take away constraint so that I'm very creative. I said: "OK guys, I'm not going to say any more. I'm leaving here, I'm going out of this room and I'm going to come back in a week with an idea that you're going to want and it's going to take you to your budget 'ouch' point!"*

I was completely making this up! But they loved it, it was like "Talk dirty!"

We went away and hatched a plan. One week later a motorbike pulls up outside these people's office and a guy gets off, a motorcycle courier, dressed in 18th century costume. He walks to the desk carrying a parcel. The parcel is wrapped in silk and inside is a handmade box of scented wood and inside that when you open it is a proposal printed in a special typeface on special paper.

And it was all to say "Look, we know we're not going to get this, but this is what happens when you challenge us."

And the proposal was "Your entire staff create an opera. You're going to write it. You're going to costume it. You're going to light it. We are going to be there to help but you will do the whole thing."

And they said Yes! The result was 1,500 of their staff performing an opera they had created in a makeshift theatre on a clifftop in Portugal.

This project led David to become creative confidante to CEOs and their teams across the world, creating over 800 experiential events for different organisations including Ericsson, Disney, Zurich and Dell Computers.

Read more about David's projects at davidpearl.net

Start a movement. When you feel strongly enough about what you're trying to do with your work, it becomes bigger than you – it becomes not just a business but a movement. What do you most want to change in your area of work? Take a stand on it and you'll attract a tribe of followers who support you. They will recruit other followers who can later become paying clients or customers.

Embrace your inner nerd. Players get passionate and even irate about their favourite topics, whether it's bad typography, poorly roasted coffee beans or ill-fitting bras. The mainstream might find your obsession odd but the likelihood is that enough other people will share it and be attracted by your passion for it. This is true in a way it never was before online marketing. Even if you have a very narrow focus, you have the entire world in which to find the tribe of people who share your interest. Create your own 'global micro-brand', as cartoonist and author Hugh Macleod calls it.

Step two: Who are your kind of people?

As you launch your project on to the world, think about who it is you most want to reach. Ultimately these people will be the ones who will pay you for what you do. When you're deciding what kind of customers, clients or fans you want to attract, your aim should be to market, sell to, and work with people you actually like.

Have you ever had the experience of trying to sell your services or products to someone you actually would rather not spend time with? I know I have. It rarely works and if you did actually win the sale, you've now entered a business relationship with someone you wouldn't choose to hang out with. When you look in your appointment diary, the reaction you should be having is, "Great, I'm looking forward to seeing them tomorrow."

Even if you're selling a product and won't have to speak to the customer again, it's still better to sell to people who are going to value what you do, get the most out of it and give you honest apprecia-tive feedback, and avoid those that want to complain for the sake of complaining.

Think about who you would absolutely love to sell your services or products to. Most people think of demographics when asked this question. How old are they? What gender? What line of work? Or for those selling to organisations: What size of turnover? What industry? It's equally, if not more important, to think about psychographics. What are their values? What do they look for in a product? Do you want to sell to people who are down-to-earth and unpretentious or people who are trailblazers in the latest trends? Do you want people who appreciate the finer things in life or who love value for money? Think about these questions and note your responses in your playbook.

From all this, imagine your ideal client or customer. It could be someone you know or someone you would like to work with. Describe them in your playbook. If it's a particular person or organisation, find a picture of them online and paste it into your playbook. When you are writing your marketing copy or email newsletter, remember this ideal person you want to reach.

Does this mean you are ruling some people out? Isn't this a crazy way to run a business? Well, the truth is you're probably already appealing to a certain kind of client or customer. All I'm suggesting is that you become more aware of it so that you can make sure the way you present and promote yourself is consistent.

What we're talking about here is niche marketing. Marketing your work is a bit like dating. You can't attract everyone. Even Scarlett Johansonn and Ryan Gosling turn some people off. It's much better to find a small group of people who find you irresistible than a huge number of people who quite like you, because there's got to be a strong attraction for someone to take out their hard-earned money and hand it over to you.

It's much easier to grow your fame within a niche. It takes real time and effort to start to get known by people. It's easier, faster and cheaper to do it within a narrower section of society or business. And you can still offer a range of services or products to that niche.

I was at a networking meeting recently when a printer stood up to give his one-minute introduction to the room and said, "I do all kinds of work for all people." How much interest do you think this attracted? Not a lot. To come back to the dating analogy, if you are single and someone came up to you and said they were looking for a relationship with anybody at all, how attractive would you find it? It smacks of desperation. People prefer specialists. If you discovered someone whose entire business is aimed at solving exactly the problem you have right now, wouldn't you be interested in talking to them?

If you're just starting out, it may take time to discover your ideal client and your exact niche. Play it out and look for the patterns as you start to work with a variety of people and projects. If you've been working for yourself for a while already, think about which have been your favourite projects and who have been your favourite clients. Could you focus on winning more of these projects or clients?

If you're still worried about narrowing your focus, realise that you might not need a huge number of customers. If you provide a service and you're selling your time on a project basis you don't need the whole world to love you, just enough people to keep you in work. And that number might be a lot smaller than you imagine. A contractor who gets repeat business from clients can survive very well on just a handful of clients.

Even if you're an artist, musician, craftsperson or author, you may be better off with a relatively small number of people that are crazy about you (and buy everything you create) than a larger number of people that are only mildly interested in you.

Step three: Choose your channel of communication

Your next step is to choose the channel (or channels) you will use to reach your fans, customers or clients. It has never been easier to reach an audience of people at little or no cost, launch your project, and build a community around it.

Would you like to have an audience of people eager to hear your latest news, support your mission or be ready to buy whatever you offer next? Your mid-to-long term aim must be to build an audience of people who have given you permission to contact them with your advice, ideas and news. Your ability to do this can make or break your mission to get paid to play. Just imagine you had a thousand fans subscribed to your newsletter or blog. That's a very useful thing when you come to releasing a new product, book or album. Send them a message announcing your new creation and you might sell some units straight away. And when you have ten thousand, it starts to get really interesting. It takes time to build a fanbase and, like compound interest on your savings, it pays to start working on it as soon as you can.

There are now many channels you can use to reach people, from simple email to your social media profiles to private online groups. You can use Facebook, Instagram, Twitter, YouTube, LinkedIn and other social media platforms to engage people, spread the word about what you do, get input and feedback, and even allow people to take your stuff and build on it in new ways (as we saw with Deadmau5). When you get it right, you'll find people using their own social profiles to market you, your business, or your cause to each other.

Authenticity and integrity are the new currencies. Everyone knows what it's really like to work with you: from roofers to airlines, because the conversation about you is being held online in public. That can include real-time reviews: people tweeting or livestreaming while still at your conference or event. You can't expect to short-change your customers and get away with it, as some large corporations have found out to their surprise. The trend is towards transparency. We can all follow the daily life of the business leaders, presidents of countries, and rock stars you used to only see from afar.

The question for you is, which channel do you want to use to play out your project? Read on to understand some of the best options.

Email

The first method people used to communicate with a mass of people on the internet was, of course, email. And it's still a very useful thing to have an email list of people interested in your work. Even social media marketing campaigns will often encourage people to enter their email address as the first step to becoming a customer. That's because email gives you a direct, private line into people's to do list.

To build one, use an online newsletter system to manage the database and send email newsletters (don't start cc'ing hundreds of people with your usual email program). The service should show you how to place a sign-up box on your website. Encourage your fans or potential customers to give you their email address in exchange for giving them something of value. This might be a quick cheatsheet or checklist you've created as a PDF or access to a focused audio or video lesson that addresses a need they have. Every week or two, send an email to subscribers with something useful to them. When relevant, include a link at the end to something you offer. Make sure people can unsubscribe themselves whenever they want, and never add anyone to an email database without their permission – that's just rude.

While we're on the subject of email, a note about your own email address: Don't run your business on a free email address like hotmail – it looks unprofessional. It's best, in fact, not to use your email address from your Internet Service Provider either, because one day you might want to change provider and you'll lose the address. Instead, purchase your own domain name to use so that your email address becomes yourname@yourbusiness.com. (If you already have a domain for your website, set up your email on that.)

Read more about email marketing at fworkletsplay.com and start collecting email addresses today. You won't regret it.

On Facebook you can use Pages, your personal profile and Facebook groups for marketing. Posts on Facebook pages tend to get shown only to a small proportion of the people who liked the page unless you pay for wider reach. Post on your personal profile about your projects and you'll often reach more people and get more interaction than on a page. Set the posts to 'Public' rather than friends only if you're comfortable with it so that anyone can see them without having to friend you.

Facebook groups are a great way to build a community of like-minded people, share images, ideas and videos, and promote events. In some ways it's as valuable as having an email list. A group allows you to get close to your supporters and potential customers, find out what they really want and start to help them out.

Instagram is very visual and has a younger demographic than Facebook. It's good for building visibility of your brand and you can occasionally post an offer in your stories for something that people can access for free by entering their email address. Once they have given you their email and permission to contact them, you can see if they are interested in a related offer for something you are selling.

Twitter is a great place to connect and build relationships. Follow and interact with journalists and leaders in your field. Share insights into your area of interest and curate other people's news by retweeting their best tweets. You can tweet me on @johnsw.

LinkedIn is the network to use if you want to sell services or products to corporations or to corporate employees. LinkedIn has had a reputation for being full of grey middle-aged men in suits posting rather dry content but it is increasingly loosening up. If you work for yourself, make sure your profile clearly says who you help and what you do. Then post useful and interesting content and interact with others. Don't do cheesy things like messaging people to have a sales conversation; wait for people to engage with you and ask for your help. If you are consistent in posting and interacting, it will happen.

Blogging

While blogging doesn't have the buzz around it that it did a few years ago, it is still useful for sharing longer articles. Whether you have your own blog, write on medium.com or publish articles directly on LinkedIn, depends on your project and your audience. Gain readers by sharing your blog posts on your social media profiles like Twitter and LinkedIn.

You can use blogging to play out your idea and detail your thoughts on your topic. While some bloggers go on to win massive book deals and other opportunities, I suggest you don't do it for the money but because you enjoy it (and ironically you'll be more likely to get famous as a result).

Even if no one ever reads your blog except you and your mum, if you go through the process of writing ten posts over a month or two, your knowledge on your subject will have deepened, your writing will have improved and your thinking on your topic will have moved forward. And if you focus your blog on something interesting with a unique slant, you will find that others will want to follow you as you play with your topic.

Over 4 million blog posts are published every single day. So how can you possibly write anything new? You don't need to. When you write in your own authentic voice, you are already unique. There is never going to be another exact copy of you with your talents, skills and experiences. If you create good content with your own style, you will attract the readers who resonate with it.

POWER-UP: Broadcast yourself

Video is a very powerful medium for connecting and marketing because it gives a much more intimate sense of who you are than a written post can ever do. For a lot of us the thought of talking to camera is stressful but if you're willing to stretch yourself you can practise recording videos and you will get better and become more relaxed about it.

Here are some basic pointers to quickly raise the quality of your videos:

1. Use the camera built into your smartphone – any recent phone has a remarkably good camera.

2. Check the lighting. Don't stand with the sun or a window behind you because the camera will automatically reduce the brightness leaving your face very dark.

3. Check the scene that's in shot behind you. When you're focusing on how you look, it's all too easy to miss the fact that you left your washing drying at the back of the room! Viewers notice these things even when you don't.

4. Get the camera level with your eyes. Avoid staring down into your laptop's webcam on the table for instance which can make you look scary. Try to look at the camera lens and not the image of yourself on the screen.

5. Don't script everything you're going to say. You know your subject area so just put three or four bullet points on a sticky note and place it next to the camera.

6. Keep your first videos short and snappy. Don't ramble. Cover one key thing you think people will find interesting or useful and finish.

Once you're more comfortable with video, try going live on Facebook, Twitter, Instagram or LinkedIn. Going live gives you the chance to interact with people during your video and answer their questions. Get the habit of using video and eventually you'll be able to go live to a million people (as I have done) with no plan beyond your handful of bullet points.

Podcasts

If you're camera shy, try an audio podcast instead. Audio gives you some of the intimacy of video without having the extra concerns about lighting and scenery. There are a lot of podcasts out there now but if you have an interesting niche or an engaging presenting style you will still attract listeners. Recording a podcast featuring interviews with interesting people is also a great way to build your network. You can listen to The Ideas Lab podcast featuring experts on turning ideas into successful businesses, brands, books and movements at theIdeasLab.org/podcast.

How to publish a book, host a radio show, or launch your own TV station in one afternoon

For every branch of the traditional media, there is now an online alternative that you can control yourself. Nothing now stands in the way between you and your fans. You don't need a broadcaster or publisher to give you permission to reach your audience. We own the media, let's use it. If you haven't checked recently, you will be stunned at just what you can do in one afternoon using services on the net that are cheap or even free.

You can publish your own book on Kindle or paperback through Amazon. This includes print-on-demand services where your book is printed and delivered directly when each customer buys it (and you keep the profit after the cost of production).

If you've always dreamed of being a radio host, start a podcast as we saw above. Or you can launch your own TV channel on YouTube.

Package your photos into beautiful photobooks on Blurb. Share your music on SoundCloud or Bandcamp. Create an event and find attendees using Facebook events or Meetup.com. Start your import business with an eBay shop. Open your own retail shop today: upload your designs to Zazzle or Spreadshirt and make them instantly available to buyers anywhere in the world as a T-shirt, mug, notebook, calendar or clock. If you hand-make art or crafts, sell it on Etsy.com, the handmade marketplace. Whatever it is you want to do, you can now launch it in some form in one afternoon. What are you waiting for?

Decide the channel you will use to play out your project. If your head is now spinning with all the options, keep it simple and pick a social media network you already know. You can always add other channels later.

Step four: Start the conversation

Once you've chosen your channel and know your people, what should you share? Your first email newsletter, blogs, social media posts or videos could simply share the problems you are aiming to address or perhaps communicate your particular angle on the field you're going to be working on. Another good thing to do is share your story of what drew you into this subject area.

Write in your own natural voice as there's no need to switch into formal business-speak. There is value in keeping it short. The shorter your writing or video, the more people will bother to read it or watch it.

POWER-UP: How to be everywhere

The human brain has a number of cognitive biases that influence our thinking and decision-making. One of them is called the 'mere-exposure effect', a psychological phenomenon by which we tend to develop a preference for things merely because we are familiar with them. On top of that there is the recency effect where more recent information is better remembered and receives greater weight in forming a judgment than information presented earlier. The upshot of all this is that the people you see most frequently in your social media occupy a larger space in your mind. And as long as you resonate with their style and content you are more likely to turn to them as a source of solutions.

That means that it really does pay to share content frequently. The most visible people post daily or multiple times a day. You might start just by posting twice a week. Whatever it is, set a schedule and stick to it. Don't be your industry's best kept secret. The key is to stop thinking it all needs to be perfectly produced videos and well thought out blog posts. You might post a funny meme or a link to a news story combined with a sentence of explanation from you on why this is so apposite to the area you work in.

Some posts can just be to elicit interaction from people. Pose a hot-button question related to your work and find out what people think. All you need to do is write "Mac or PC; what should I buy?" and stand back and watch the fireworks.

Your job then is to keep yourself at the front of your followers' minds by keeping in touch with regular content, posts and emails. This takes persistence and that's why it's so important you choose something you're genuinely interested in. I get

▶

people taking my programmes two years after I first met them because they've been receiving my emails every week or following my Facebook posts. What are the chances they would have remembered me without this?

This is not about posting endless promotional messages (which would get irritating very quickly). Send things of real value. There's enough spam and sales junk on the internet. Add to the signal not to the noise. Share news, expert tips, engage your followers, canvas their opinions, offer to answer their questions online, run competitions. You might choose to directly address the problems you identified in the last Secret to work on. Ask people what their experience is of this problem and what solutions they've found. Or if you already know something that helps with this problem, explain it. You can also get some great content by interviewing interesting or well-known people in your field. Don't be afraid to give away your best ideas and content. Rather than losing you business, this will actually attract a lot more.

Beyond this, just sharing your own journey to create your project can be very engaging. There's no need to pretend to be more expert or more successful than you are. Share what you're learning as you go. If you manage to bag a meeting with a personal hero, people are as interested in the video you record on the way to meet them and your honest sharing of your excitement and nervousness as they are in what you find out from them.

Don't just post your stuff and run – respond to comments and ensure you engage with other people's content too. Liking, favouriting, commenting, or sending someone a private message or email saying how much you liked what they just put out, builds connections and relationships. Some of the people you connect with might share your posts or agree to partner with you to share your content on their channel or website with a link back to you. This can bring you a flood of new people instantly.

Keep creating value for others – that means putting out stuff that educates, entertains, interests or helps those in your target market.

Don't turn into some slick marketer or sleazy sales machine. Be a mensch. Help people, take an interest, find out what's on the minds of your audience. Be you, complete with your doubts and weaknesses – share your challenges and how you overcome them as much as your rave successes. The corporate world encourages us to hide our flaws or quirky personality traits but in today's world this is exactly what we fall in love with in our heroes and role models from Elon Musk to Oprah Winfrey. How can you really be yourself in a way that supports your business?

The era of the picture-perfect influencer is coming to an end. Our heroes now are authentic people with good hearts who know their flaws so that we can feel more comfortable with our own. "Vulnerability is the new sexy" as Jeetendr Sehdev told me, author of *The Kim Kardashian Principle: Why Shameless Sells (And How to Do It Right)*, on The Ideas Lab podcast.

Step five: The art of seduction, or how to turn your fans into customers

Now you've started the conversation with the people you want to reach, how do you attract them towards buying your products or hiring you? First, think from your reader's perspective when you're communicating with them. People starting out in business for themselves tend to talk about how they do their work or what features their products have but this is really not that interesting to the person looking to buy. They're more interested in the benefits or results they can expect from your service or product. But there's something even more powerful than this when you first want to get your readers' attention: it's to talk about the problems you identified them as having.

There's a famous phrase in advertising that says, 'Enter the conversation already going on in your customer's head.' Your customer or client's inner conversation is often about what's bugging them most: 'I've tried everything and I still can't get rid of this back pain', 'Why can't I find a TV that I can actually operate?', 'These mortgage payments are killing me', 'Why are all tie designs so boring?' When you write a blog post or email newsletter that addresses your readers' problems, you grab their attention.

Once you have their attention, don't try to convert your fans into buyers in one step. To return to our dating analogy, you can't really go up to someone who barely knows you and say, "Hi, you look nice. Do you want to get married and have three kids?" Similarly in business, you shouldn't expect to convert strangers into buyers in one step. Instead, draw them step-by-step into a deeper relationship with you.

They might start by following you on social media, then giving their email address in exchange for a free guide you've created. If they like that, they might spend a little money with you to buy a small product or taster session. Some of the people that do that will go on to buy something more significant from you or hire you personally.

At each stage of this dance of seduction, make it clear what you want your quarry to do next. Spell out what the next step is with a clear 'call to action'. When someone has read your website, what's the very next step you want them to take? Expecting them to pick up the phone might be too much of a jump. Perhaps the best next step is to entice them to give you their email address so that you can put them on your mailing list. You can then send them an email that tells them about a free talk you are giving. Each step draws them closer into relationship with you.

Make it obvious what you want them to do. If you send out an email saying to get in contact, that's actually too vague. Do you want them to email you? Call you? End the email by putting the number right there: Call me on 0800 . . . You will be amazed how simple things like this will increase your success. My local independent cinema is currently raising funds for renovation. I ran into the manager who was brainstorming ways to find £140,000 within eight weeks. The first thing I did was look at the front page of its website. Where was the notice to ask people to donate? It was in tiny italicised writing buried in a small box of five recent news stories. He took my point and added a wide banner across the top of the website. If you want someone to do something, make it as easy as possible for them.

Coping with controversy

Listen to your own tastes. Be prepared to be unpopular.

Abraham Maslow, American psychologist, 1908–70

Once you dare to take a stand and give up the anonymity of the crowd, don't be surprised if you piss some people off. In fact, if this doesn't happen, you're probably playing it too safe (particularly if you're trying to change the status quo). Remember that to turn some people on, you have to turn other people off. As long as you are an amorphous blob, no one can take offence. Once you define yourself, you will polarise people for you or against you.

Ray Charles once said his mother gave him two excellent pieces of advice: 'Always be yourself' and 'Not everyone is gonna like you.' It really doesn't matter what your topic is or which stand you take, someone won't like it. I've seen people angrily attack others on topics as diverse as stone masonry, knitting, and how to be happy. No one is immune, so accept that it's part of the life of being a player.

Everyone has the right to disagree with you. What's more troubling is when someone turns that into a personal attack on you. Remember that if the strength of someone's reaction seems to be wildly out of proportion to what you did, then accept that it is not actually about you and what you said. It's more likely that you've triggered their emotional baggage.

If someone makes an unpleasant personal attack on you, you have two choices. You may choose to simply ignore it (and perhaps block them). Avoid getting drawn into arguments with people who are simply looking for attention. On the other hand, if they have posted something publicly that misrepresents you or your work, you might want to challenge it before leaving the conversation. And if anyone makes threats towards you online do report them. These things happen a lot less than you might imagine and are only likely to become a problem when you become very well known.

Remember that what you give your energy to tends to grow – don't give it to conflict. There is a danger for all of us that the negative responses get stuck in our head while all the positive feedback passes us by. Start to do the opposite by collecting all the appreciations, encouraging comments and good reviews that come your way.

Now you know how to start to attract your own fanbase, in the next Secret you'll find out how to offer them something irresistible.

Put it into play

Keys to this secret:

➡ Pimp your project – dare to stand out.

➡ Describe your ideal client or customer.

➡ Choose your channels of communication to reach your audience.

➡ Start the conversation and keep in touch.

➡ Attract your fans towards becoming paying customers.

What you should have now:

➡ A chosen channel to start communicating.

➡ A description of your ideal client or customer.

➡ Some ideas about how to start the conversation.

Take ten minutes to play:

➡ Go share something on your chosen communication channel that you think might be interesting or useful to your target audience.

Exclusive extras on fworkletsplay.com:

➡ My recommended services for blogs and websites.

➡ Podcast interviews with David Pearl, and experts on personal branding, LinkedIn, and email newsletters.

Secret seven
How to create an irresistible offer

The companies that survive longest are the ones that work out what they uniquely can give to the world, not just through growth or money but their excellence, their respect for others, or their ability to make people happy. Some call those things a soul.

Charles Handy, management expert and author

You've now seen how to use digital marketing to get yourself known for what you do. You've also seen how to define the people you want to be known by. The question now is what will you offer them. We looked earlier at how important it is to know the problems you want to help people with. This Secret will help you work out what solution you can provide for those problems and what form to deliver it in. Once you know that, you'll have something to offer that allows you to get paid to play. When you get it right you can find you have something very successful on your hands as Adam Wilder did.

Creating the world's first 'festival of authentic connection'

Adam Wilder is founder of Togetherness, helping a world of increasingly isolated individuals explore meaningful connection with themselves and others. I interviewed him for The Ideas Lab podcast to ask him how he created his first big event, The Togetherness Festival.

I've had a number of businesses and projects since my 20s and they have always involved creating experiences of richer, more enjoyable contact with each other. I ran the biggest Burns night in Europe. I did a hot tub bar in Hackney Wick. I did immersive comedy in an old Victorian cemetery in East London. I've always been interested in people relating more deeply.

But I found it really exhausting to have different brands and different audiences that didn't join up, each with different ways of communicating to their audience. And I wanted to just have one thing that I could focus all my energy on. I didn't know what it would look like, I just had vague thoughts of a festival to bring everything together.

The real catalyst was actually going to someone else's festival in London and it had workshops and courses that I think were good, but I really didn't like the way they did it. I thought it was way too pseudo-spiritual and pseudo-scientific. Though the content was on the whole good, I felt they were doing it in a way in which less than 1% of people will take to it and everyone else is going to find really weird. And I just had this very, very strong feeling that I knew how I would do it differently. I decided pretty much there and then that I was going to create something. And so that's what I did. I called it the Togetherness Festival, the world's first festival of authentic human connection, and I planned it for six months. I didn't know what I was going to do afterwards but I just thought I'm going to run this festival. We can do it in London and we're going to make it really accessible for people who don't do this kind of thing normally. The venue I found was at the top of a skyscraper in the Canary Wharf financial district.

I got in touch with the teachers that I think are really brilliant and interesting. Our curation was really good. There were talks and workshops about relationships, about sexuality, about the language we use and how it affects our work, and about the science of psychedelics for depression.

But I also think one of the most important things with events is to make people feel welcome when they arrive. I mean, when I go to an event, I feel a bit nervous if I don't know people, so I tied the whole thing up with a lovely welcome and a nice way to help people to meet each other.

And it worked fantastically. We sold all 500 tickets, we were featured in The Guardian *newspaper, we did great. It actually made a profit. And there was a big sense that wow, this is something that people love and get stuff from and want to continue. And so based on that, I then developed everything else we now do at Togetherness.*

Read more about Togetherness at togetherness.com

Getting paid to play means doing something you really enjoy while providing something people are happy to pay for. Your job now is to find something you can offer that people really want. And what people really want are solutions to their problems. Look back at the list of problems you wrote down in Secret five. What can you offer that solves these problems or at least goes some way towards helping with them? What results can you promise for people who have this problem? Remember that it's the results people are really paying for when they buy your product or service.

People don't want to buy a quarter-inch drill. They want a quarter-inch hole!

Theodore Levitt, Harvard Business School marketing professor

The clearer you can be on the results you provide, the easier it will be to get paid for them. Here are some examples. If you're a virtual assistant helping clients with the problem of being too busy to organise their business appointments and sales meetings, you could solve it by doing all of it for them. The result for your clients could be more business – and more money coming in.

If you're a hypnotherapist you could address the common problem of fear of flying. The result for the client is that they can finally travel further afield to warmer holiday destinations, enjoy the journey, and arrive already relaxed.

If you run a blog about Bali-inspired interior design and you import related crafts and furniture, you can solve the problem for people who love the Bali style but don't know how to create it in their own home. The result for your readers and customers could be a beautiful lounge or bedroom featuring some of your unique pieces not found anywhere else in the West.

The more significant your results and the more impact you have on the problem, the more valuable you are. And the more valuable you are, the more you can get paid. If the problem you address is boredom at work, you can have a small impact, like making people laugh for a few minutes with a funny blog. In which case you might make a fraction of a penny per person off advertising. Or you can provide someone a complete out-of-the-box business opportunity to allow them to escape their job altogether. In which case you can charge hundreds or thousands of pounds.

Your natural instinct as a beginning entrepreneur might be to explain in detail how you work with people: how many sessions the buyer will get, what your product is made out of, or the name of the therapeutic approach you use. But this is not what makes people buy. What makes people buy is the difference you can make to their lives. Right now they have a problem in some area of their life or work (or at least some dissatisfaction), as we discovered in Secret five. That is what is driving them to look for a solution. And if they can see that their life will be better in some way (even if it's just a little) after they've bought your product or service, making the sale should be easy.

I call this 'Makeover marketing' because the most important things to describe on your website or marketing materials are the *before* and *after*. The before is their life right now with the thing they want to change. The after is the difference you've made to their situation after they've had the results you provide.

Once you know what the results are that you provide, the question then is how you deliver them. You could provide your results by offering a physical product, a printed book, an online information source, or you might do it by working with the client directly. You can provide a similar result in lots of different ways. Adam Wilder for example runs Togetherness live events, holds a silent dating night called Shhh Dating, creates experiences for other people's festivals and events, and is creating online courses.

POWER-UP: Find the perfect offer

If you want to get going quickly, your final choice of offer should aim to hit the sweetspot between three Ps:

1. **Play:** What feels in flow for you? What excites you? What kind of people would you be happy to work with as a target market?

2. **Practised:** Choose something that uses your existing skills, knowledge and talents. What areas do you have a lot of expertise or skill in? What do people rave about when they work with you?

3. **Profit:** What do people have a clear problem in and so are motivated to find a solution? What are people happy to pay for? What is a good market to approach that has money?

You might not know this sweetspot for yourself immediately but if you get out there and start being helpful to people you will be able find it.

How to turn what you know into your own business

Many of us now have a career that pays us primarily for our knowledge and expertise. We are not working with our hands and we don't need to be chained to an office to deliver the value we provide.

What's really exciting is that today there are so many more ways to turn what we know into a business. Here are some of the ways to provide your knowledge and expertise as part of your own business. None of these have the hassle of running a full-blown business requiring staff and premises or a large financial investment.

In fact, even if you're currently looking to find another job rather than go self-employed, you might find that experimenting with one of these channels helps you to create your next role (we'll look at this in greater depth in a later Secret).

Providing a service

A lot of people start their journey into self-employment by providing a service to individuals, groups or organisations and charging for it by the hour, day, week or project.

People who charge by the hour include counsellors, life coaches, complementary therapists, accountants and plumbers. Contractors and consultants often charge by the day. Others such as web designers and software developers might charge by the project. There are now some people who charge by the minute and websites like Clarity.fm exist to help you do exactly that.

Advantages

If you have the skill, this can be the fastest way to turn your value into money. There is no complex business plan to write, no premises or systems to organise. It can be a good place to start because it puts you in direct contact with your target market so you get a sense of what's on their mind, what their problems are and what they want. This knowledge can support you in later creating a product or business to deliver the same results without needing to work with them directly – something that allows you to make more money without working more billable hours.

If you have specialist skills that are in high demand, you can earn a good income compared to similar people in a job. With a high enough rate, you can afford to take some time off in between projects.

Disadvantages

Selling your time is like running on a hamster wheel: you can get going straight away; the money's fine while you're working but as soon as you stop, the money's gone. Also, it can be difficult to find time to win your next client while you are on a project. It can end up feeling pretty much like a job. When you factor in unpaid holidays, sick leave, training time and times when you can't find any work, you find your annual income is not as great as it first appeared. And if you want to get really rich, this is not a good route because you only have a limited number of hours per month you can charge out. You won't see anyone in the annual rich lists who sells their time.

In addition, even people with strong skills are finding themselves commoditised – the available competition of a global marketplace for expertise is creating a downward pressure on prices.

Ways to make it work for you

When working on a project basis, if you can charge enough for your time, you can start to take time off between engagements. Rather than 'Time is money' this means 'Money is time'. The more you charge, the more time you can take off. If you can earn four times your living expenses, then for every month worked you can take three months off to do other things – go travelling, write your book, create a course.

Some people work this model very well. There are IT contractors who do a six-month contract and then take six months off to travel the world. Ultimately, if you do not enjoy the paid work then you are not getting paid to play. You simply end up dreading your return to work. Worse than this, you have to spend some of your time off marketing and selling yourself into work you don't really want. Remember the aim is to find a supporting income stream that is enjoyable.

Here is a great tip for you on the other hand if you're going to sell your time by the hour. If you sell every hour individually, you may end up talking to a prospective client for 30 minutes to sell them one hour of your time. Instead, package a number of hours into a solution and add in other items like physical products or online instructional content.

For example, a massage therapist, rather than selling a one-hour massage for £65, can sell the 'Ultimate recovery package' aimed at people recovering from a stressful period at work or at home. It might include three massages, a hypnosis CD to destress, a printed booklet on changing stress-inducing thoughts, and some relaxing essential oil to use at home – all for £195. Not everyone will go for it, but some will buy it just as readily as the one-hour offering. Packaging your services in this way can make them much easier to sell, particularly if you can clearly quantify who it is for and the results they can expect from it.

Ultimately the best solution to commodisation and the need to make more money is to build a unique brand and business around your skills. So instead of being yet another project manager, digital marketer or yoga teacher, you create a unique offer that is the perfect solution for a very specific problem. That makes you the go-to person for anyone who needs it. (I run something called the Pioneer Programme to address this exact problem.)

Consultants are hired for their specialist expertise for durations of a few days to a few months. They often charge by the day and can be paid thousands of pounds a day depending on their target industry and their standing in the market. My experience of being an independent consultant is that although people hired me for my specialist expertise, many times that expertise simply allowed me to understand their language and their business. A lot of what I provided was actually common sense. I would ask everyone involved what was going wrong, what they thought would work better, assess it all based on my experience and write it all up in a report. The answers to a company's problems are often available right there within the company itself, so don't imagine you always need to bring some radical new insight.

There is no doubt that corporate consulting and training can pay very well. Daily rates of £2,000+ are not unusual. When I quit my corporate job to go into independent consultancy, my aim was to achieve a daily rate of twice that from my former salary with benefits so that I could take about half the year off. In the end I was able to quadruple that rate meaning I only needed three months of consultancy work per year to make what I used to make in my job.

Bear in mind that it's not always the most skilled person who gets the work. Never underestimate the value of simply being around at the right time and being a likable and reliable person to work with. I've been hired purely, as someone explained, because "I know you'll do the work on time" (even if they didn't know that I worked late into the night to finish it).

If you have a good level of expertise in an industry and you would enjoy being involved with cutting-edge projects, start going to conferences and networking events and meet people who could hire you. 'Consultant' is a very broad label. It really pays to know the problems you help with and the solutions you can provide so you can communicate just what you do for clients. A good way to start is to fill a recognised role like project manager or technical architect.

A good play project for you if you're looking to move into consultancy is to write a white paper – an article demonstrating cutting-edge thought on a current hot topic. Post it on your website but also on LinkedIn and other platforms where your target customer hangs out. Also follow the advice in 'How to be everywhere' in the previous Secret and make a habit of sharing content daily about your area of expertise.

Ebooks

Ebooks are one of several ways of 'canning' your knowledge for people to absorb. An ebook can either be published on Kindle or simply delivered as a downloadable PDF from your website. The advantage of publishing your ebook on Amazon is that 6 million people visit their site every day searching for something to purchase.

When you consider that you might only make 50 pence from a traditional book sold through a publisher, earning £10 or more from an ebook suddenly looks very appealing. However, you will need to do all the marketing to help people find your ebook on Amazon.

It's easy to create ebooks as a PDF and make them downloadable on your website. All word processor apps can now output to a PDF. A focused PDF ebook that addresses a specific problem for your audience can be useful as a free marketing tool (as people provide their email address) or as a low-price product that might get people interested in working more closely with you.

Online courses

Online courses are a great way to provide some of your expertise as an interactive experience without you turning up. There is currently a lot of hype about making money from these courses and while it is possible to do so you can't simply throw a course up online and sit back and wait for the money to roll in.

In reality the people who make six figures or more from courses as I do, live and breathe their subject. They are creating multiple courses and consulting offers all aimed at the same target market and they put out daily free content on the same topics, as we discussed in Secret six in how to be everywhere.

As mentioned previously, unless you are already well established in an industry with a large following, I recommend you run your course the first time as a much more interactive, high-touch experience. That means you deliver the content live, perhaps in a Facebook group instead of an online learning management system. You might create a programme somewhere between three and six weeks long, deliver the content live each week as an online presentation, and set people tasks and answer their questions in the group as you go along.

This way you get to test out your material and get a huge amount of feedback about what people value in it and where they get lost. Once you have this feedback you can turn the same content into a do-it-yourself course online. Or you could continue to run it as a live programme if you prefer.

Membership programmes

A membership (or continuation) programme is any income stream where you charge customers at regular intervals, most often monthly. In return, you provide useful information, training and support on your topic of expertise. This could be on how to train dogs, how to change career, how to set up your first online shop and so on. Membership programmes give you the chance to have a deeper and longer-term connection with your customers. Sometimes they operate as a community around a common interest.

Gateway Women

Jody Day started a community called Gateway Women during a course she did with me a few years ago. Jody wanted to help women like herself who were childless not through choice. Many childless women (who didn't choose to be) report feeling undervalued by society, which is particularly painful if they are also having feelings of grief at not having had children. Jody felt strongly about this and as a trainee psychotherapist at the time, she was keen to do something to help others. She coined the term 'Gateway Women' because a gateway is a threshold that can either be a closed door or an opening to something new. She started by finding the courage to tell her own story in a blog post. Then she volunteered to give a talk at a networking event. There Jody met a journalist who wrote about her ideas in *The Guardian* newspaper. This brought women from all over the world looking to connect and share their experience. Jody had discovered an unspoken problem that wasn't being well addressed by others and as a result she found herself spearheading a movement.

Gateway Women has now touched millions of women's lives around the world and her private Gateway Women online community gives ongoing support to over 500 members who pay an affordable monthly fee.

Find out more about Gateway Women at gateway-women.com

In business terms, membership programmes are exciting because once you've convinced someone of the value of being a member, they will continue paying you until they actively unsubscribe. Imagine you charge £20 a month, and in return you provide monthly live training, and answer questions in between in an online group. If you can attract a hundred members, that's £2,000 a month of revenue. Find 500 and you're making £10,000 a month. Many people charge a lot more than £20. (Charge £29 a month and if you manage to sustain membership of 3,000 people, you'll make over a million pounds a year.) As ever, you need to provide great value, be able to attract a lot of potential customers, and then effectively communicate the results members can expect so that they want to join.

If you can write valuable content regularly as discussed before, and start to attract a good number of followers, you are in a good position to offer a membership option with exclusive content or tuition. If you don't have enough content or expertise yourself, you can bring in other experts.

Advantages

The great advantage of membership programmes is the ability to make the sale once and get paid repeatedly. They are a great addition to other things you might offer, such as online courses or consultancies.

Disadvantages

It's one thing to sell people a membership programme but no matter how good it is some people will still leave every month. That means you need to keep winning new members to sustain the revenue. In addition, running a membership programme means you are committing to the ongoing delivery of content and help to your members. Be sure to choose a membership you'll enjoy spending time with and a topic that fascinates you.

Affiliate marketing – selling a product without having to make it

Another way of making money is to promote other people's solutions on commission, otherwise known as affiliate marketing. This works best when you've already built up a significant following.

If you see something that would be very helpful to your audience such as an online course or programme you could arrange with its creator to become an affiliate. They'll provide you with a unique tracking link. Send an email to your followers describing why you recommend the product for them, include your tracking link, and you'll get paid each time someone buys. Make sure you trust the person concerned and their product or you will destroy the trust you have built up with your audience.

It's possible to create an entire business around affiliate marketing. For instance, you can create a blog on a specific topic and include affiliate links in some of your blog posts. Don't think of this as an easy route to wealth though. You'll need to be good at search engine optimisation and online marketing and create a lot of content.

Other ways to deliver your solution

There are lots of other ways you can deliver solutions to people's problems: run events and workshops; create a software application (or hire someone to do it on upwork.com); or you can develop an online service which charges for usage or makes money through advertising. Whatever it is, find a way to play it out, experiment with it, and use the techniques in Secret four 'How to guarantee your success' to ask advice from people who know the specific challenges and strategies of this kind of project.

Many successful businesses use a combination of all these ways to deliver value. For instance, you can read my ideas in my books, take my online programmes, attend occasional live events, or work me with me in a private client mentorship.

How to make money in your sleep: the wonders of passive income

If you've spent your whole life turning up somewhere in order to get paid, it can be a dramatic shift to start thinking about getting paid without being there. Passive income is income from a project that once you've set it up, keeps paying you without any further work. Think of royalties on a book or a song you've written.

When you earn your first piece of income without being present, it is quite a thrill. I remember waking up one morning to read an email telling me that that while I was asleep someone had paid £97 for a downloadable audio programme from my website. The recording had already been automatically delivered to the buyer without me needing to do anything. It's a small sum, but it was without doubt the best £97 I had ever earned. (Fortunately the amounts have grown somewhat since then.)

Passive income is a subject of much hype. In reality, almost no income is 100% passive. If you're selling online courses you have to spend time building the audience who will buy it. When you've written your book, you have to promote it. Even if you own a property to let out and have an agency manage the tenants, you will still occasionally have to talk to them when something unexpected comes up. I prefer to call this 'low-maintenance income'.

What most people really want in their business is scalable recurring income – money that comes in each month without having to panic about going out and selling something. This is what smart entrepreneurs focus their attention on rather than expecting to make money for nothing. If you like the people you're working with and enjoy what you're creating in the world, why would you want to stop doing it? No one's really working a four-hour working week, not even Tim Ferriss. Why would he? He loves what he does.

POWER-UP: How to create raving fans

We've talked a lot about solving problems but there is another aspect to creating irresistible offers – ones that people rave about to their friends. And that's the category of 'Warm Fuzzies', or making people feel good.

If people have a fun experience working with you or taking your course, that counts for a lot. And if they come away feeling better about themselves than they did before that's even more powerful. Purchases are largely made because the buyer believes it will make them feel better – safer, smarter, happier, sexier, less afraid, more fulfilled.

Give people not just practical help but a wonderful experience and they will tell others. That's free marketing for you. Give them a reason to feel better about themselves and it will be life-changing. Adam Wilder did this at his first Togetherness Festival by making sure that not only were the speakers interesting but that everyone felt very welcome and comfortable at the event. And they went away feeling a little less of the isolation many of us can feel at times in a busy city like London. That's why Adam has people who come back again and again to his events – whether it's to his one-day festivals, his silent *Shhh Dating* events or volunteering to take part in breaking the world record for the number of people spooning together.

Remember from the principles of being in flow and the Belbin team roles in Secret two that you don't have to provide everything in your solution yourself. You can hire or partner with people to provide content, do the technical stuff, spread the message, make sales or anything else that is a weakness for you.

You now have the basic formula for getting paid to play. If you can deliver a great solution to a pressing problem, communicate the results you provide for people, and provide it at a price people are happy to pay, you will have created an irresistible offer. In the next Secret we'll look at how to launch your offer on to the world and win your first playcheque.

Put it into play

Keys to this secret:

➡ Know the results you want to create for people.

➡ Choose a way to deliver to those results: freelancing, consulting, online course, membership programme, and so on.

What you should have now:

➡ Something to offer the people you most want to work with.

Take ten minutes to play:

➡ Start writing something that describes your offer (often referred to as a sales letter or sales page in marketing terms): describe the problem you address, the results you provide, how you deliver those results, and why you are capable of doing this – your training, experience, and any testimonials to back you up. Also think about how much you want to charge for it.

➡ Arrange to show this to potential customers or clients and get some feedback. Once it looks good enough, place it on your website or use it in emails and on flyers.

Exclusive extras on fworkletsplay.com:

➡ More about offering services like freelancing and consulting.

➡ Podcast interviews with Adam Wilder of Togetherness plus other examples of people who consult to corporations, run online businesses or have created a successful personal brand around their expertise.

Secret eight
How to win your first playcheque

The secret of living is to find people who will pay you money to do what you would pay to do – if you had the money.

Sarah Caldwell 1924–2006, Opera conductor and founder of the Boston Opera Group

You've now seen how to get yourself known and how to offer something that people really want. Now it's time to put it all into practice and actually make some money. This Secret will show you how to win your first playcheque and prove you can get paid to play. Remember that being a player means that you are creating your work – there is no job for someone to hand you and no standard formula to getting paid. But if you are determined, persistent and willing to think creatively, there will be a way to get the experience you want from your work.

Here's how Dan Barker made his transition to getting paid to play.

Winning a first playcheque as photographer

Dan Barker was in aerospace engineering working as a stress engineer just a few years ago when he realised he wanted a change. As Dan explains:

> *I read* Screw Work, Let's Play *several years ago when I was feeling fed up with my job and trying to figure out what to do. I used some of the exercises suggested and they kickstarted my journey to where I am now.*

> *For example, I wrote out what I would do if I had a year off and money was not a problem. I did that exercise several times and*

*then looked for the common threads. I also put aside one after-
noon each week as dedicated 'play time'.*

*My wife was super supportive and because we were living in a
very small place at the time, she took the kids out to town every
Friday afternoon (the place I worked finished at 12 on a Friday)
so I could 'play'. I tried several things, playing with some 3D
printing for example. I also used this time to carry on reading
your book. I remember one Friday feeling really pumped after
reading about doing something you love. I got up, grabbed my
camera and went out to take some pictures. Previously I'd been
a bit shy of using my camera out and about, but after reading
that chapter, I just got out there and didn't care what anyone
thought. I felt liberated.*

*I still remember the first time I earned money from photography
and it made me realise it was possible. My wife was in the local
wine shop and they mentioned they were having a website built.
The owner said they had to photograph all their stock and had
no idea where to begin. So she said I might be able to have a
go. I went in and had a chat with them and we agreed that I'd
see what I could do. I had no idea how to photograph wine
bottles and I only had basic kit. But I researched it as much as
I could online and spoke to a photographer friend I knew to ask
his advice. Critically, the idea was that I'd go in and have a go,
but there was no pressure on it. If it didn't work, no worries, if it
did work we'd discuss it.*

*So I went in, set up and produced some reasonable results. Cer-
tainly good enough for them, they were happy. I realised that day
that it only has to be good enough for your client, not be the best
wine bottle photograph ever produced in the history of photography. We discussed the final images and how they should look
and I put forward a price (on a 'per bottle' basis). It was very low,
but it felt good to be earning money from photography.*

I still shoot for them, seven years on, and they've been really supportive. I think they've enjoyed seeing me grow the business and get out of my job. One thing I've found is that when you tell people what you want to do, they get behind you.

Dan also joined my private client mentorship for a few months and still uses the website and brand we developed during the sessions.

I've since been on a journey to build my photography business and managed to leave my job 18 months ago. I've had a great year, and in several of the months I've already made more than my old monthly salary.

Read more about Dan's work at danbarkerstudios.com

You don't have to try to get paid for every play project you undertake. You can of course carve some time out of your leisure time for some of them. But if you're reading this book, you ultimately want to do more than just create a hobby crammed into the spare time smeared around your day job. Getting paid for your playing means you can do more of it, and you can start to tip the balance away from the work you don't enjoy to the things that feel like play. Money makes play sustainable – it allows you to keep playing.

As comedian Eddie Izzard says, "I'm not a capitalist, I am a creativist. I want to make money so that I can create things." As long as you are getting paid for something other than your play project (e.g. a day job), you will always be splitting your time, attention and energy.

As soon as we start talking about money, you might be tempted to get all 'serious' and 'practical' and make some terrible compromises in your choice of project. This is the problem with the whole area of work – we've been trained to take whatever we can get when this really isn't necessary any more.

You know you're on the right track when you would do the central part of your work for free because it is so much fun. We looked at what this is for you in Secret one. If you can solve problems for people while doing this, there will be a way to monetise it, that is, make an income.

Myth 12: You can't get paid for doing what you love

A lot of people believe the myth that you simply can't get paid for doing what you love, despite the fact that people all over the world do just that. Whatever it is that you'd like to do, you can bet that someone somewhere in the world makes their living out of doing exactly that.

It's true that some things are far more competitive or take longer to get established. Writing a novel or making money from your own music for instance are extremely challenging. Ultimately it's your choice how much time and effort you want to put into something.

More often than not though, there will be a path that enables you to be in flow, enjoy what you're doing and get paid for it. And when you choose the right path, you'll enjoy the journey. What this means is that as soon as you start, you've already arrived – you're a success. Being a success is really just finding a sustainable way to do something you love and really care about.

If you have the habit of dabbling with lots of possible money-making ideas and never following them through to the final step to actually make a return, then it's time to do something different. Take your project all the way to the point where you can sell it at least once. The income may only be small but it's an important symbol of your ability to turn something you've created into real money.

But I need some money right now!

Making money from a completely new line of work is likely to take some time. During your transition, you'll probably need another source of income. If you're currently in a job you're keen to get out of, pause for a moment and check whether you can give your job a makeover to make it more enjoyable while you're creating a new line of work elsewhere.

My client Susan decided after a number of sessions that it would be best for her to stay in her current job a little longer. We had been working on how to find something more creative for her. I asked her if she had told her boss the kind of work she really wanted to do and she admitted she hadn't. The next day she spoke to her boss and explained she wanted more work using her creative writing and sense of design. Her boss said, "That's great, we need someone to work on the brochures and the website. Would that suit?" Susan was delighted.

Can you give your current job a makeover in a way that makes it a better fit while you find something completely new? Can you take on new responsibilities that will help you when you finally do escape to something else? Can you go part time while you transition?

If you're already self-employed, the quickest way to make some income is to look at something that you can do that you're already qualified for and experienced in. The problem is you might find that you suddenly can't seem to get the work you used to do. I often see this in my work with clients. They decide they'll do one more contract or temp job to bolster their bank balance before they quit for good but strangely can't seem to get it. Why? Because once you've lost your enthusiasm and you've psychologically moved on, somehow people can just pick it up – even when you try your hardest to appear keen. You just can't fake enthusiasm. And if you try, you'll find yourself competing against someone else who genuinely wants the work. Guess who'll get it?

Even if this is an area of work you're looking to escape eventually, take a moment to look for a piece of it that is most appealing. What's your favourite kind of project or role in this area? Focus your search for income in this area. Your enthusiasm will help you win it and it'll be more enjoyable when you do. Alternatively, if you know you can survive for six to twelve months without much income, and you know what you want to do next, perhaps it's time to cut your losses and start building your new life.

I see people get into a mess when they get all their possible future paths jumbled up – whether it's staying in their current work, starting their own business, or pursuing their artistic passion. The best approach is to separate these out. If you want to be an artist, do it now in any spare time you carve out around your job – use microblocking if necessary – and don't assume you must turn it into your main career. If you want to start a business, explore the options, get to know your target market, create your offer and ideally win and deliver your first sales in your spare time before you think about quitting. More on this later.

Bear in mind that if your new venture requires developing whole new skills (rather than using all the skills and knowledge you've developed in your current work), it will take longer to get off the ground. That's OK if it's what you really want to do.

Winning your first playcheque

Earning your very first income for doing something you love is an important landmark – it's your first playcheque. You may find it takes more effort to get your first sale than for the next ten added together. Or you may find it drops in your lap seemingly without effort.

As mentioned, win your first playcheque while still in your current work if you possibly can. This means you're still being paid during the first few months when you might not be making much from your play yet. This has the added advantage that you will have less of the air of desperation about you compared with the person who needs the new income to survive.

Getting paid for your play project is the best way to prove its value to others. Once people are paying you, it means you have found product/market fit in start-up terminology. You've found a way to package what you do in a way that meets an existing need and people are happy to pay for.

Myth 13: All my friends have said they would buy what I'm offering, so I must be on the right track

Asking your friends if they'd buy what you're offering is not market-testing. Getting paid is a far better test that you are on the right track than the positive comments of your family and friends. It's important to have the encouragement of those nearest to you but it's not the basis for a business. The only real test for whether people will buy something is to sell it to them – and at the actual price you will need to charge for it to make you a living. People will say all sorts of nice things about how they would buy what you're creating but unless they reach for their wallet and hand you their money for it, it's not enough.

It's appropriate that you might start out by charging less when you have limited experience or your product is still in rough form, but you need to know that there is a way further down the line to make the money you need.

A note about working for free

When you're just starting out, it's no bad thing to do some work for free. If you have a chance to do exactly what you love most and get better at it in the process, do so. Any opportunity early on to experience being in flow, doing that thing you were born to do, is worth taking. It also connects you with your target market and provides a wealth of information on their wants and needs.

Look for a fair exchange of value. It doesn't have to be money. If someone offers you a chance to demonstrate your skill in front of a large audience of prospective customers, this can be a great marketing opportunity. You might give a free talk at a conference or write an article for a magazine. The results from this kind of exposure can be more effective than paid advertising – and all it costs is your time.

If you're continuing to work for free because you're afraid of charging properly, it's time to bite the bullet and get professional. Providing something for free does not constitute market-testing – everyone likes free. Even if you're still training in the skill you are practising, it's a good discipline to charge at least a token amount. This puts things on a professional footing. Also, people don't value things that are free. The drop-out rate for free events for instance is huge – 60% or even greater. Charging even a small amount dramatically increases people's commitment so that they are more likely to turn up – and to do so on time.

Myth 14: I can't possibly charge for what I'm doing yet – I need to read more books and take more courses and workshops

This myth is often just fear in disguise. Books, workshops and training courses are great to build your skills and keep you motivated but don't use them as an excuse not to get started. Start small and don't overpromise.

Run a campaign

To win your first playcheque, run a campaign. This works really well if you're aiming to land a job or sell your services as a freelancer, consultant or independent professional. It can also be modified to help you win your first large product order or your first agent, reseller or supplier, as we saw in Charlie and Harry Thuillier's story in Secret four.

Say you want to launch yourself as a web designer or virtual assistant or you want to sell your homemade cosmetics or foodstuff to a supermarket. Your first step is to have a clear offer as we saw in Secret seven and to know your ideal client or customer as we discovered in Secret six. Then make it a play project to throw all your energy and effort into getting exactly the work you want to do with the people you want to work with. This is not the time to make wild compromises. Don't assume that by spreading your net wider you improve your chances. You don't. By spreading your focus, you weaken the effect. Compare a laser to a floodlight. They are equally bright but the laser focuses all its power into a tiny point. This gives it the strength to cut through paper and even metal. When you focus a lot of energy in a single place, you'll be surprised just what you can achieve.

My escape from the world of jobs

My early career was in technology innovation for the broadcast industry. When I first chose to become an independent consultant, I decided I would like to work for the BBC. It seemed to be doing the most interesting work in my area, I liked the friendly people I had met there, it was the best-known broadcaster in the world (I like to work for the best) and it had been something of a childhood dream of mine to work for them.

While still in my job, I called everyone I knew who worked in or around the BBC. I also called all my colleagues in the rest of the industry and asked them if they knew of anyone inside the BBC who might be able to hire me. I emailed all the people that might be able to help that I had email addresses for. I read the latest news on the projects the BBC were running and sometimes cold-called people who were mentioned in the news reports.

And after three months I'd had several discussions, email exchanges and meetings and . . . still no consulting contract. I had now left my job with nothing else on the horizon. Finally, one morning while I was still in bed, I got a call on my mobile phone, "Hi. I'm calling from a division of the BBC, can you come in for an interview today?" I started my first contract the following Monday helping on a cutting edge, multi-million pound technology project.

When you're starting out on your own, it can sometimes take months of pushing before you get noticed. As long as you are getting engagement and interest from the people you talk to, don't be surprised if it doesn't pay off immediately.

Notice the feedback you're getting and be willing to fine-tune your campaign according to the response you get. Be ready for the fact that even with the best planning in the world, taking expert advice, and following your own instincts, your grand launch into a new line of work sometimes falls flat on its face on its first attempt. It's what you do next that will determine your success. Will you give up or make some changes and try again?

Get specific

Be clear what you'd like. Be specific enough to land an opportunity you will enjoy but not so specific that you make it near impossible to find it.

The benefits of being specific

Back when I was working as a developer on special effects software, I went on a careers workshop and a couple of people there asked me to help them find work in my company. A woman called Sarah asked me if I could find out if there was any work going. I asked what work and she said, "Anything at all". A second person, David, told me he wanted to be a special effects artist and asked if I could ask around at work for someone who could give him some advice.

Who do you think I could help the most? Sarah's request was so vague I didn't know what to do with it. David's request was easier to deal with because it was more specific. I went and spoke to some of the people at work involved in the special effects industry and asked their advice which I then passed back to David. When you're asking for help, keep your questions specific.

Write your killer email

Write an email covering the following:

➡ What you're looking to do and who for. If you're working for yourself rather than going for a job, this is where knowing the problem you solve and what solution you are offering is very helpful.

➡ What you bring that is of value to the people who will hire you (skills, knowledge, experience, any previous high-profile clients or jobs).

➡ Why you're particularly keen to work with this kind of organisation or person. Sometimes a little flattery (if it's genuine and it's tastefully done) can be very helpful.

Keep the email as short as possible. The shorter the email, the more likely recipients are to read it. Then send it to everyone you know who you think would be willing to help. Ask them in the email to forward it to anyone else that they think could help.

If you're better on the phone or in person, make use of that too, but the advantage of email is that if you do it well it can spread beyond your group of friends and colleagues. A personal Facebook post can also work.

Myth 15: I can't talk to anyone until I have launched my website and have a good logo

This is nonsense. It is almost always possible for you to win your first playcheque before you have a website, business cards or much of the other paraphernalia of self-employment. Don't use those things as an excuse. You can always type up a one-page brochure and send it by email. Remember that your first sale is likely to be a contact from a friend or colleague so they will hopefully be more forgiving that you're not yet professionally polished. Business cards are overrated anyway. Most cards handed out to people are never looked at again. It's much more important you take someone else's card if you're interested in selling your services or products to them. At least then you're in control of getting in contact. But many people now simply don't have a business card.

If instead of trying to get hired you want to offer a course, package or product of your own, you can write a killer email describing your offer and send it to any followers you have built up. If you don't yet have many followers you can ask someone to share it with their audience as we discussed in Secret seven.

POWER-UP: How to fix a flop

Have you gone out to the world with great excitement and been met with nothing but silence? Here's what to do when your ideas have fallen flat. Ask yourself these three questions:

1. **Is your offer too vague?** Have you defined exactly who you want to buy? Have you then designed a specific product or service that those people want? For instance, if you are currently simply offering your services for use by anybody, can you specialise in a particular niche or offer a solution to a real problem people have? Sometimes the best thing you can do at the start is to 'superniche' – solve a very specific problem really well. What could that be for you?

2. **Are you guessing what people want?** It's great to do something you're passionate about but the key to getting paid to play is to do what you love in a way that provides something people value. If you don't know what that is, go and ask them. Find out what your target market wants, what they are worried about, what they want in a solution, how they describe their situation, and what else they've tried before (see Secret five). Then you can be sure of offering something they'll happily pay for.

3. **Have you put the effort in?** The early days of getting something off the ground can be *hard*. You can't expect to simply send an email, write one social media post and see your venture take off. Approach everybody who could possibly be interested and tell them what you're doing – even if that means individually emailing or calling dozens of people. Decide now that you will do whatever it takes to get paid to do something you love – and be willing to be flexible to make it work.

When you get there, celebrate!

When you win your first playcheque, whether it's selling your first online course, session or artwork, or winning your first freelance project or contract, pause for a moment and celebrate. You just got paid to play. Don't just brush it off because you're still a long way off making enough to live on. Go celebrate with some friends or with your support team.

Your first experience probably wasn't ideal. It might not be quite what you really want to get paid for, you might not be happy with what you produced or what you got paid and it might have been nerve-wracking or a bit of an anti-climax. That's OK. Just carry on, notice the feedback and how it feels to do it and keep adjusting to aim for the thing that's the most fun and the most rewarding.

In the next Secret you'll find out how to scale up this first experiment to get paid to play full time.

Put it into play

Keys to this secret:

➡ Look for opportunities to be in flow – do what you're good at and enjoy doing.

➡ Run a campaign to win your first playcheque.

➡ When you get there, celebrate!

What you should have now:

➡ A plan for your killer email to win your first playcheque.

Take ten minutes to play:

➡ Using the offer you created in the last Secret, start crafting your killer email to send.

Exclusive extras on fworkletsplay.com:

➡ Interviews with people explaining how they won their first playcheques.
➡ Details of my free 5-Day Business Startup Challenge to find a business idea, create an offer, and even attempt to win your first playcheque in 5 days.

Secret nine
How to play full time

I never did a day's work in my life. It was all fun.

Thomas Edison

In the previous Secret you saw how to win your very first play-cheque. This Secret will show you how to scale this up and move towards getting paid to play full time. To do this you've got to do something good enough to generate word-of-mouth recommendations.

Spreading the word

Derek Sivers was a professional musician when he founded CD Baby, which then went on to become the largest online retailer of independent music. His advice here for musicians is equally relevant to artists, writers or entrepreneurs.

> When people say "Hey man, how do I get my music out there?", I say "Well, what do your friends think of it? And do they like it enough that they have told all of their friends about it?" When friends hear your music they should say "Oh my God! This is really good. I want to send this to a friend of mine." And they want to do it for their own sake, not for your sake. That's impor-tant. You don't want to have that thing where you're asking friends to help promote you as some kind of favour to you as a friend. They have to want to spread the word the same way that somebody who saw the Mentos and Diet Coke video on You-Tube thinks it's hilarious and wants to send it to their friends. It has to be that same impulse.

The bottom line on scaling up your project is that there has to be excitement on both sides – you're excited by what you're doing but what you're doing is also exciting other people.

What's your next step after winning your first playcheque? It's to do it again and prove your first sale wasn't just a fluke. Find yourself a group of test subjects, or guinea pigs, to repeat the process with. If you can find ten people who love what you're offering so much that they want more of it and they spontaneously rave about it to other people, then you've hit the jackpot. As marketing guru Seth Godin wrote on his blog about this very topic, "If they love it, they'll each find you ten more people (or a hundred or a thousand or, perhaps just three). Repeat. If they don't love it, you need a new product. Start over." Until you can find ten people who are excited by your work, all the marketing tricks in the world won't help you.

There isn't such a great mystery as to who's going to be a success and who isn't. Are you getting clear signals that the world (or at least the little bit of it you are interested in) wants more of what you're offering? If not, take a moment to reflect on what you need to change. Are you still doing something that you're not really that keen on? Are you offering something people don't really need (check it solves a problem)? Are you offering it to the wrong people? Or are you enjoying it but you're just not good enough at it yet? If so, stick at it. Consider getting other people in to guide you or to do the bits that you're not so strong at yet. You don't even have to be the person that creates the product or delivers the service. Perhaps your skill is in marketing the idea you've had, or building the systems to support it or doing the deals to win the work. Then collaborate with others to create the product or deliver the work.

You'll know when you've got something good because others will tell you.

The moment Leslie Scott realised her game Jenga was going to be a hit

When Leslie Scott was in her twenties, she borrowed her baby brother's wooden bricks and invented a game with them. She built a tower of bricks and challenged friends to remove blocks without collapsing the tower. People found the game really compelling and then she told me:

> Early on, I played Jenga with professional sportspeople at a fund-raising event and they loved the game. I woke up the next morning thinking you just show this game to people and they love it and get totally hooked on it and I thought well maybe I should start a business and put the game on the market.

Leslie decided to get some sets manufactured to sell, calling the game 'Jenga' derived from the Swahili word kujenga meaning to build. It was a long and challenging journey to launch the game and at one point she ran into considerable debt.

> This chap turned up, knocked on the door, and explained that I hadn't kept up with the payments on the car so he'd come to take it away. My attitude at the time was something like "Oh dear, I quite liked that car, but I can live without it." He was quite surprised when I invited him in for a cup of tea before he took it away.

Leslie survived the debt and the bailiffs and after several years signed a deal with Hasbro, a multinational toy manufacturer. Jenga has now sold over 80 million units and is in the top three most popular games in the world along with Monopoly and Scrabble.

Leslie didn't stop there though.

> I've since designed and published forty games, none as commercially successful as Jenga but just as fun and exciting to

create. Getting something on the market that never existed before is exciting. I wouldn't have done any of this if it hadn't been challenging and fun to do. And when the fun stops, it's time to move on.

Once you've won your first paycheque and repeated the experience with ten people who love what you do, you can start to scale it up. Let's look at the different ways you can get paid to play full time. You don't have to restrict yourself to just one of these. You might choose to develop several strands and income streams. The question now is, simply, which one do you want to start with?

The job 2.0

The conventional job is not a good vehicle for getting paid to play. The problem is that you have to fit into a shape carved out by someone else. It's very difficult to get into flow because it doesn't go down very well in a job if you say, "I don't like doing that task, so I'm not going to do it."

The good news is that there is an alternative to the old-fashioned one-size-fits-all job. It's the customised job: Job 2.0, if you will. A customised job is one that you create from scratch or, at least, shape yourself. It's what happens when you come at the world of the job with the player's mindset and ask, "What do I want to create for myself? What value can I bring?" Here's how to create one: think of what your ideal work would be (based on your thinking so far in your playbook), consider who would find this most valuable, and then run a campaign as shown earlier to go speak to them. Avoid job adverts, recruitment agencies and HR departments.

Myth 16: I've been applying for jobs and talking to agencies and I've got nowhere, so it must be impossible

It's said that up to 70% of jobs are unadvertised. The rest are filled through personal connections. Jobs filled by this route are often more flexible than ones that are advertised and screened by HR departments. Recruitment agencies rarely help you change career because they mainly make their money from filling vacancies as quickly as possible and will look for the closest match with the greatest experience. Small companies are usually more flexible than large ones. This means that they are likely to be more open to negotiating on what your role will be, what experience you need, and the structure you will work in. If you can impress them enough, you should be able to shape or even create the role you are seeking.

But if the jobs are not advertised, how do you find them? Find ways to hang out with people who are in the industry and particularly those who are in a position to give you work. Remember that if you love this industry or type of work, you should enjoy going to their networking meetings, conferences and events. Get seen. Play the fame game to get noticed. Make it a play project to run an event, or a networking meeting, freelance at an exhibition, write a blog about this world or interview its thought leaders.

How I created the last three customised jobs I had before starting my own business

1. I interviewed at a small software company advertising two jobs I was interested in and I asked that they combine them into one job for me. They agreed.

2. I met someone involved in setting up a new ebusiness consultancy. (I met him at an interview for a different job that I did not

get and did not particularly want.) I continued to speak to him for a period of six months as the new company took shape. I suspect he never actually read my CV. He later said, "I just knew you would be good for the company." I ended up as Chief Technology Officer of a division of a very friendly and creative start-up.

3. A small group of us moved as a team from a small company to a global consultancy. In this case, someone with experience of the world of recruitment arranged meetings with the largest companies in our industry. We were eventually hired as a team to start a new service line.

The great thing about this process is that when you deliberately seek out your ideal job, your enthusiasm shines through in the hiring process. Now imagine the tables were turned and you were in a position to hire someone. Wouldn't you be more interested in someone who had sought you out especially and explained why they were keen to work for your organisation in particular?

The customised job rarely gives you quite the same flexibility as self-employment to sculpt your working life exactly how you want it. The advantage, however, is that you don't have to worry about marketing yourself. If your final destination is still self-employment, the customised job can be a good stepping stone on your way out of the job market. A part-time customised job can also be a useful part of a portfolio career. It often provides more of a team experience than self-employment does. And if you really have terrible self-discipline, a boss is a useful thing.

Going freestyle

The miserable history of work is represented by the uninspired vocabulary we have to describe it. We need a new word for the kind of lives we are creating now. 'Self-employed' is something found on a tax form, business man or woman brings an image of a grey person in a conservative suit talking in corporate speak. 'Entrepreneur' is a word that beginners have a problem identifying with.

None of these words explain the whole reason for leaving the world of jobs – freedom, autonomy, self-expression, fun, the chance to finally create something only you can create. Author Barbara Winter calls us 'joyfully jobless', Daniel Pink calls us the 'free agent nation'. I think of it as going freestyle.

This encompasses freelancing, consulting, coaching, advising, and anything else where you can start making a living without a job and without necessarily needing to form a company (rules on this vary from country to country).

If you haven't tried working outside of a job before, it can seem like a huge leap and you might be labouring under the popular myths surrounding it. Here are two of the most common.

Myth 17: It's safer to have a job than to be self-employed

If you're still in a job right now, you might find your colleagues warning how much safer it is to stay in a job. But in fact, as an employee, you can be fired or made redundant at any time with as little as a month's notice and little or no redundancy pay. A job is actually rather like being self-employed but with only one client: your boss. When you're self-employed you will have several or even hundreds of clients. You're very unlikely to get fired by all your clients at the same time. The risky bit is making the jump without testing and winning some clients first, which we've already seen how to avoid.

Myth 18: I'd be crazy to go self-employed in the current economic climate

When the economy is on a downturn, it certainly makes sense to test out your ideas before you jump from your current employment. However, don't assume that you should give up on self-employment altogether. People still make money in a downturn, and in fact some businesses do better. If you can save people money by providing something they need in a cheaper way, you could even get rich. The supermarkets that are perceived as cheapest (such as Aldi and Lidl) experienced a boom after the 2008 banking crisis.

On the flipside, the richest consumers tend to be insulated from fluctuations in the economy so it might be the right time to move up market and offer something to the most affluent in society (think Wholefoods). Learn from the wisest people in your field and watch what they do.

Starting a scalable business

I'm not a businessman; I'm a business, man!

Jay-Z, American rapper, record executive and entrepreneur

Another way to get paid to play is to create your own scalable business. That means that instead of selling your time by the hour, day or month, you build something that can serve more people and make more money without a comparable increase in work.

This might be an app, a membership programme, or network of events run by people you train. We looked at the kinds of things you can offer to achieve this in Secret seven. Creating something scalable requires longer-term thinking, the ability to delegate, and a scaling plan that uses systems or people to multiply the impact you're having. We'll look more at this in the next Secret.

Myth 19: I need an original idea to start a business

This is the myth of the great invention. Why is it as soon as we start a business we imagine we must invent a new kind of vacuum cleaner or an app that's never been tried before? Programmes like *Dragons' Den* promote this idea. If you are actually an inventor and have been playing with inventions for as long as you can remember, keep inventing. For the rest of us, just take a look down your local high street. How many hairdressers are there? How many bars are there? How many newsagents? Instead of looking for a new idea no one's thought of before, look for a problem or niche that isn't being well served right now and address it. Stamping your business with your personality or your own unique spin on a topic is a great thing to do (and something I love helping clients with), but bear in mind the actual skills you use and activities you undertake in your business are likely to be exactly the same as many others'.

Most important of all, do something people want and do it well, make a profit, and play the fame game intelligently.

We're lucky. Even ten years ago, the options for starting your own business were far smaller and the risks much higher. Thanks to the internet, now anyone can launch a business in a day. There are kinds of businesses you can launch that five years ago didn't even exist. What this means is that you no longer have to mortgage your house to start something. You don't even need to leave your job. You don't need to rent a shop on the high street and spend tens of thousands fitting it out. You can go online and build a shop in an afternoon – for free. Whatever grand vision you might have for your work, there is a way to start right now, in a scaled-down form, test it out and then scale it up. And there is no reason to restrict yourself to just one money-making activity.

Create your portfolio career

If you get bored easily doing just one thing, like the scanner personality we talked about earlier, you can build a portfolio career to keep you interested. There's no reason to pretend you will one day become ruthlessly focused. Instead, deliberately build a working life that has lots of variety in it. Build a portfolio of multiple income streams. Some might be selling your time, others could be online courses, affiliate marketing, or even property investment. If you want to have multiple income streams, make sure some of them are low-maintenance income as described in Secret seven. Once you've set them up, they will then continue to pay you while you start something else.

Some income streams might only make you a few hundred pounds a month. But each one you add will take you closer to your desired target while giving you plenty of variety in your work. Having more than one string to your bow can actually be safer than relying on one line of work. If the market changes suddenly, some of your income streams may suffer, others may be relatively unaffected or even boosted.

A portfolio career is not always easy to manage. The best way to make it work is to be clear which of your income streams is your cash cow and make sure you don't let it slip no matter how busy you are with other things. Even if you eventually intend to have multiple projects running concurrently, only launch one at a time. Projects require the most energy and attention when they are first launched. Get something working to a point where it doesn't need your constant attention before thinking of launching another project.

Remember that most projects you want to succeed require you to both create something and market it. Beginning entrepreneurs often put all their attention and energy on designing their product or service, not realising that you are likely to need to spend at least as much if not more time on marketing.

If the projects in your portfolio are very different and aimed at different types of people, you're going to have to put a lot of time and effort in. It is far easier if there is a common strand to what you do. Get known for something: be 'the personal brand guru', 'the builder that actually turns up', 'the coder that can communicate' or 'the friendly techie'. If you can find a theme that captures your real talent, it becomes much easier for people to understand what you do and so recommend you to other people.

Damian Barr has a remarkable portfolio career. He has written award-winning books, he's a columnist, TV presenter and playwright, he runs the Literary Salon in London and last year became the Literary Ambassador for the Savoy Hotel in London. But he told me when I interviewed him in the Savoy for The Ideas Lab podcast that the common theme in everything is a love of stories. As he put it, "Stories are my life. What am I without them? I don't want to live without them and I don't want other people to live without them. That's kind of my guiding mission."

A portfolio career is easier when you do several things for the same market of people or companies. That way, once you have become well known among internet start-ups, or women entrepreneurs over 40, or people who love to travel independently, you can easily offer them the other things you do. For example, if you get known for being a virtual assistant to busy consultants, and you then learn how to set up simple websites, you can offer your clients a special service to create their first consultancy website.

Collaborate for speed

A good way to make a large project happen quickly or to be involved in multiple projects is to collaborate with others and focus on the part you are best at (and enjoy).

Myth 20: I can't go self-employed because I'm no good at selling/marketing/IT/finances/creative ideas

You don't need to know or do everything in your business. Find other people to do the bits you're not so good at. If you love presenting but hate finance, collaborate with someone who loves spreadsheets but hates performing in front of an audience. You don't even need your own idea to start a business: you can team up with someone else who's got the good idea and bring your people skills, technical skills, sales skills or organisation skills.

Over time, there is value in learning some of the things you have been weak at – having at least a basic understanding of skills such as hiring, finance and sales is very useful in entrepreneurship even if you are going to find someone else to do the bulk of the work.

A lot of people make the mistake of collaborating with people who are too similar – you're both very extrovert and big-picture oriented, or you're both introverted geeks. This leaves big holes in your capabilities. If you're both geeks, who's going to do the sales and marketing? If you're both loaded with ideas, who's going to turn them into a plan and a timeline you can follow?

To be really successful you will need to collaborate with very different personalities. As entrepreneur and business coach Judith Morgan says, "You have to work with people who irritate you." As an introvert you might find the sales guy kind of showy and over the top, and he might find you a bit dull and serious. As long as there's enough mutual respect, it could be a good combination. Think back to the Belbin team roles in Secret two and look at the descriptions of the roles and notice where you are weakest. Collaborate with someone who can fill those holes for you.

POWER-UP: Partner with others to bring you a rush of new business

Once you've got something good to offer as confirmed by your first few customers or clients, how do you get enough people to come to you to make it into a real business? You can start following the guidelines of Secret six to get famous but this does take time. Rather than purely relying on building your own audience one person at a time, you can get a rush of new people coming to you with this well-used business trick: get more well-established people to market you. Imagine someone with an email list of 100,000 people writing about your business in their newsletter, or promoting you to their large Instagram following, or inviting you to speak in a room of hundreds of your ideal clients. All these things are possible but how do you do it?

First, make sure you know the problem you solve and who you solve it for. Now ask yourself: Where do these people hang out? What do they read? Who do they follow online? What email newsletters do they receive? What events do they attend? Whose other products do they buy?

Once you know, work out how you can put yourself in front of these people. Can you write an article for a website or a magazine that you know your ideal client will be reading? Or give a talk to an audience of just the right kind of people? Or ask someone with an email database of thousands of the right people to mention your new product? You can offer to do the same in return or pay them a commission on the sales you make.

Finding my first 2,000 email subscribers

At the beginning of my journey helping people to build creative careers and businesses, I ran across a company in a similar area. Careershifters had been founded a couple of years before by British entrepreneur Richard Alderson to support people making a major career change. At first I thought they were a competitor and had a moment of jealousy looking at their slick website and impressive PR reach, before I had either of these things. Then I realised we were actually complementary to each other. My focus was increasingly helping people start their own thing and Careershifters was about changing career.

I got in touch to see if there was some way we could work together. Richard invited me to help run their workshops with another coach. At the end of the workshops I passed round a clipboard with a sign-up sheet. I emailed everyone with my free downloads to help choose the right business to start and added them to my newsletter. I also started writing advice articles for the Careershifters website and included a link to my free toolkit at the end of each article. Both these activities were unpaid for me at the time but they gave me invaluable experience working closely with people on their journey to starting something. Equally important, partnering with the company in this way provided my first 2,000 email subscribers, many of whom went on to be paying clients.

You could call this a win, win, win situation – Richard and his colleagues got free content and coaches for their workshops, the Careershifters audience got useful advice and workshops, and I gained experience and email subscribers. Who could you partner with in a similar way?

So yes, continue sharing content and building your own network but also take every opportunity you can to borrow someone else's network.

Do the numbers work?

Before you go much further, let's check that the numbers add up.

Myth 21: I need a 30-page business plan before I can start

In the early stages of getting paid to play, you really don't need a formal business plan. It is, however, a very good idea to do a back-of-an-envelope calculation for your own benefit. I call this 'The 3-line business plan'.

Here's the version of the 3-line business plan if you're selling a service. Think about your desired monthly income. Then estimate what you think the average client or project will pay you. Divide your desired income by this number and you know how many clients, projects and sales you need per month. Now check, can you actually service this number of sales in a month? Remember that it takes time to find clients and you also need to put aside time for training, administration and so on.

If you're selling physical products, work out your profit on each product and then calculate how many you will have to sell to make your desired income. You can quickly come to appreciate why finding someone to sell your products in bulk is very important.

If you're selling online courses or other digital products, your income will equal the number of website visitors multiplied by the percentage of visitors who buy multiplied by the price of the product (less any commission or payment processing fees). Just realise that your percentage of buyers might be 1% or less. Don't forget that there will probably be multiple income streams to factor into these calculations.

Since you might need to live on less while you're getting set up, it's important to know what the minimum income is that covers your basic expenses without the frills. Then know what a comfortable income is that you could sustain for longer and also work out what your desired income is. You might be surprised how few people do these simple sums. They're important to look at because they'll affect your choice of business. If you need £100,000 to survive, you might need to rule out some options you would consider if you only needed £25,000 a year.

When to quit your day job

Don't be too quick to jump from the work that's currently providing your income. Better to gain momentum first while still being paid elsewhere. Being stressed about money is not a state conducive to playfulness.

Once you know that the numbers work, you've proved that people want what you're offering and you have more demand than you can service in your spare time, you may well be ready to jump.

Taking redundancy can help you make your escape. If a redundancy programme has begun where you work (or there are rumours of one), be clear on your position: do you want to leave or not? Don't just wait and see what happens. Make up your mind, then see if you can manoeuvre yourself into or out of the firing line accordingly.

Once redundancy is offered, remember that the terms can be negotiable even when it doesn't look like it. Always ask if you want to modify your leaving date a bit or keep a benefit like a company car for a while. You'd be surprised how often you can get this. You may think you have nothing in your hand to negotiate with, but most companies want to part on good terms so will be open to sweetening the process if they can. If redundancies aren't on offer, it may still be possible to negotiate favourable terms for your departure such as paid 'gardening leave'.

How long is all this going to take?

Malcolm Gladwell famously made the argument that it takes 10,000 hours, or approximately six years full time, to become a world-class success at something. However, his examples were of concert musicians and professional sportspeople. You can't accidentally practise the violin or your backstroke in your everyday life. But you can build your skills in speaking, negotiating, persuading and understanding your field of interest as you go about your daily life. Every time you read a book that fascinates you, have a passionate discussion with someone, or get a kick out of getting the best deal on your travel trip, you are practising skills and building knowledge that could be a part of what you turn into your career or business. That's why building it around the things you love doing is so powerful – because you tend to do the things you love a lot, so you get good at them.

In fact, I would say you're already a world-class expert. At what? You're an expert at being you. No one does *you* better. You've spent your whole life doing it and you get good at what you do a lot. Whatever your moment of magic is, you've been doing it since you were a young child: talking to people, making people laugh, cheering people up, reading and writing, drawing, studying, organising, negotiating, savouring food, enjoying nature, patching relationships up. All this practice has built circuits in your brain that others just don't have. You see the world differently. If you've been performing and telling jokes to friends and family as long as you can remember, but you've never done any formal public speaking then you need to learn the practical skills like timing, story structure and so on. But you're not starting from scratch. If you love doing something, you're almost certainly already doing it somewhere in your life even if you don't recognise it.

Focus on mining these natural talents, develop your skills around them, and look out for a common theme in everything you do that you can really commit to. The theme might be a certain kind of person or segment of the market that you help. It might be one thing you are known for doing well (as we saw earlier in portfolio careers). It could be an overarching problem you are set on addressing (from Secret five), or it might be a brand you have created. When you find your theme and really commit to it, people sense it and you start to attract the opportunities and income you want. It might even make you rich, as we'll see in the next Secret.

Put it into play

Keys to this secret:

➡ Run your offer again with a group of ten test subjects.

➡ Are people raving about you yet? If not, keep adjusting and improving until they do.

➡ Decide your route to playing full time: the customised job, freestyle career, scalable business or portfolio career.

➡ Collaborate with others for speed and to enable you to manage a portfolio of projects.

➡ Check the numbers work before you go any further.

What you should have now:

→ A strategy for scaling up your first test-run to something that could work as a full-time living.

Take ten minutes to play:

→ Allow yourself to daydream a little about the point when you are getting paid to play full time. Describe what your portfolio of work looks like in your playbook.

→ Brainstorm ways you can collaborate with other people to make this daydream come true a little faster.

Exclusive extras on fworkletsplay.com:

→ Listen to audio recordings of my interview with Derek Sivers, the founder of CD Baby, Leslie Scott, creator of Jenga, and Damian Barr of the Literary Salon.

Secret ten

How to play your way to the rich life

You can get everything in life you want if you will just help enough other people to get what they want.

Zig Ziglar, American author and speaker

In the previous Secret we saw how to scale up what you offer to get paid to play full time. So is it possible to get *rich* from playing? This Secret will help you work out what rich actually means to you and get you a little closer to it sooner than you might think.

There are plenty of players who have turned their experimental projects into major ventures with international reach. Harry and Charlie Thuillier have raised over a million pounds of funding for Oppo, inspired by living off wild foods found in Brazil. David Crane turned a curiosity for psychology into a #1 app with 4 million downloads. Sam Bompas and Harry Parr turned wacky experiments with breathable cocktails and architectural jellies into an international 20-person flavour studio.

Derek Sivers turned fiddling around on the web to selling his own music into a business that made over $100 million in sales. Leslie Scott turned a game using her baby brother's wooden blocks into one of the world's best-selling games but says, "I wouldn't have done any of this if it hadn't been challenging and fun to do."

The principle here is to create wealth from providing genuine value to the world. When you have proven that you can do that in a repeatable way as shown in the preceding Secrets, the challenge is then how to scale up to provide more value to more people.

If you think getting rich is all about profit at any cost, you're choosing the wrong role models. When your wealth is based on providing real value, everybody wins. Building personal wealth goes hand in hand with extending the positive impact you are having. Elon Musk has said that after he exited PayPal with $180 million "I thought 'Well, what are some of the other problems that are likely to most affect the future of humanity?' Not from the perspective, 'What's the best way to make money?'" The result was SpaceX, Tesla and Solar City – and a personal net worth today of $43 billion.

Players are driven by what they want to create as much as anything else. As Anita Roddick, founder of the Body Shop, once said, "Entrepreneurs want to create a livelihood from an idea that has obsessed them. Money will grease the wheels, but becoming a millionaire is not the aim of the true entrepreneur. In fact, most entrepreneurs I know don't give a damn about the accumulation of money. What gets their juices going is seeing how far an idea can go." Ironically, it's exactly this attitude that often leads to the greatest financial rewards.

Creating real wealth from your play takes plenty of time and effort but if you master the following five keys, you should make the journey a little smoother and a little shorter.

Create your vision of the rich life

What does 'rich' actually mean to you? You might be thinking of a certain amount of money but in fact isn't it really about experiencing a different kind of lifestyle, a rich life? Think about what your rich life would look like. What would be different for you? What would you own? What are the experiences you would like wealth to provide for you?

Write it down in your playbook and find images to represent it. Putting your focus on the experience rather than a number allows you to find creative ways to get what you want sooner. If you want to have a mansion in France, you might find a way to have at least some of that experience very soon without becoming a millionaire. Perhaps you could find a place on a house-sitting site, or you could rent the house to run a workshop or conference in and so have other people pay you to be there.

Don't put off your happiness until you reach your financial goals. Savour moments in your life that represent what you want more of. Recently I found myself having lunch with a friend outside a Thai restaurant in the London sunshine. As we sipped lemongrass tea and discussed her imminent move to America to further her acting, the conversation turned to money and doing what you love. I said that I was feeling rich right then – because if I had a million pounds in the bank, I wouldn't choose to be doing anything different. I'd still be sitting with some good company eating tasty Thai food in the sunshine. So you could say that I am already rich (and the whole experience only cost us £15 each).

Catch yourself feeling rich. Notice those moments when there is nothing else you need, nowhere else you should be, and no one else you would rather be with, because in that moment you too are already rich.

If you can't enjoy what you have, you can't enjoy more of it.

Richard Bandler, co-creator of neuro-linguistic programming

If you can't appreciate the rich moments you are having right now, you might discover you won't be able to appreciate it if and when you really do achieve your financial dreams. We've all seen the millionaires who just can't stop. However much money they get, whatever they buy, they never seem to appreciate it and never feel satisfied. That's not happiness.

And of course, the other reason to appreciate how rich you already are is because it tends to attract more of the same, which means you'll realise those financial dreams all the sooner. People like to hang out with happy people and they like to hire those who look like they're thriving. In fact, the less you look like you need the work and the less available you appear to be, the more people want you – they assume you must be good!

Is your rich life about the freedom to travel?

Would you like to live somewhere sunnier or be free to travel anywhere in the world? Why not start now? Since it's now possible to run a business with nothing more than a phone, a laptop and an internet connection, do you really need to stay in the country? How would you like to travel the world and still make a living? Join the growing tribe of location-independent entrepreneurs who travel the world while running their businesses from a laptop.

POWER-UP: Create a business you can run from anywhere in the world

Whether you want to travel long term like Taylor & Camille who we met at the start of the book or spend a month or two at a time in a beautiful location as I do, it's never been easier to create a career or business you can take with you.

Here are some pointers to help get you started:

➡ You will almost certainly find it easier to get your new location independent work off the ground before you go travelling. Choose a career or business centered on things you can do remotely – software development, tech skills, copywriting, online marketing, coaching and advice. There are countless freelance gigs on Upwork, Toptal, People-Per-Hour, Freelancer.com and Guru.com to get you started.

- Replace face-to-face conversations with Skype calls and group meetings with video conferences using an app like Zoom.

- Start off with a play project – perhaps a 30-day trip working remotely to test it out.

- If you want to ensure you have the company of like-minded people on your travels, head for a location with a digital nomad community or a popular co-working space. Search nomadlist.com for ideas. Bear in mind the time difference if you're going to be working with people in your home country.

- Get your vaccinations up to date and buy health insurance.

- Join Meetup.com, Facebook and WhatsApp groups of locals, ex-pats and digital nomads in the area you're going to. Not only will this help you make social connections but they are also often the best source of affordable accommodation options.

- Store your most important files on the cloud using iCloud, Dropbox or a similar service so that you automatically have a back-up if the worst should happen and your laptop is broken or lost.

- Buy a local SIM card for your phone on arrival so that you can make calls, check email and use Google Maps on the move.

It takes time to discover how you work best while travelling. After all, you're not on holiday but you do want to enjoy what's on offer in the location you've travelled to. I find that even when I'm quite busy working I still love being in Bali, Thailand, Serbia, New York or wherever I've chosen, because I'm experiencing great weather, amazing scenery, a different culture and cuisine, and I have the flexibility to see the sites between work commitments. Tonight for instance, I'll be celebrating finishing this chapter with sunset cocktails at a beach bar with 20 or more other friendly digital nomads.

Tom Hodgkinson is editor of bi-monthly magazine *The Idler* and is author of several books including *How to be Idle* and *How to be Free*. I interviewed him some years back about the working life he has created and he explained that he works from 9am to 1pm, concentrating on writing, then checks his emails before taking the rest of the afternoon off. He's free then to have lunch, read, take a nap, go for a walk, play his ukelele, or do some gardening. Instead of working relentlessly to get rich, Tom is happy to settle on a medium-level income and advocates thrift, cutting out any expense you don't really need. "Your children will think you're really mean but you'll end up having more time to play cards with them."

If your vision of a rich life is about plenty of free time and relaxation or spending it with your family rather than yachts and mansions, you can choose to structure your life accordingly. And when you start really enjoying your day-to-day life, you might find you no longer need to spend so much money on the things you used to buy to compensate for being miserable at work. When I added it up, I was shocked to realise that when I was working in a corporation, I was spending nearly a thousand pounds a year on cappuccinos – just to get me through the day.

Is your rich life about your personal growth?

For me and many other players our work is a vehicle for self-expression and the ongoing journey to know ourselves and develop ourselves.

Hunting for treasure

Petra Barran built Kerb the street food incubator and accelerator (which we saw in Secret one) into a powerhouse in London's food culture selling over 10,000 dishes a week at five markets. So where does she go from here?

By 2015 we had a team of 8 at KERB and I had come to a personal and professional crossroads. Both me and the business needed to keep growing. I realised that I wasn't the one to take KERB to the next level - it needed a different brain and a different kind of focus if it was going to reach its full potential. And I was feeling increasingly like I wanted to get out of my lane.

When I turned 40 I had a huge moment of asking myself what success actually meant. I realised I didn't simply want to continue on the same path for myself, becoming more conventionally successful but so busy focusing on growing a business that I shut off other parts of myself that felt like they needed airing.

I am struck by that Henry David Thoreau quote, "It is not enough to be busy. So are the ants. The question is: What are we busy about?" What is success anyway? I've realised it's not what the world tells you it is, it's what each of us decides it is – and that's moving confidently in the direction of your dreams.

My dream was always to live in the deep south and contribute, somehow, to the culture. I dabbled in this dream in 2014 when I lived in New Orleans for 3 months while doing my master's degree in Urban Studies and I became hooked. It's so much life, so much funk, so much flavour all up in your face, in every kind of way. It stimulated me hugely and awoke parts of me that could often lay dormant in London.

I applied for a U.S. Green Card in 2015 and received it 18 months later. Meanwhile, I looked for a 'bulldog' to run KERB for me and I am very lucky I found the wonderful, tenacious and totally committed Simon Mitchell to become CEO. We spent 18 months on the handover in London and have worked together on various parts of KERB's growth since I moved out to New Orleans in 2017. It's a pretty remarkable situation.

I'm now back to working out what I want to do next. This can come with all sorts of confusion that I long ago thought I'd left behind me - all part of the shedding of one's props! Someone recently told me "Sometimes you need to stop asking your brain and start asking your body what's right" and I think there's a lot to that. We don't give our bodies enough credit for knowing stuff and guiding us in the right direction. I've come off social media and I'm practising the underrated art of loitering to see what that helps me unearth. . . And when people ask me what I'm doing now I say "I'm hunting for treasure".

Read more about Kerb at www.kerbfood.com

Is your rich life about the power to change the world for the better?

If so, the model for you may be to create a social enterprise: an organisation that applies commercial strategies to achieve a social or environmental purpose. The power of this model is financial sustainability. Rather than relying on a continual campaign for more donations or government funding, the enterprise generates profits that can be reinvested to further your mission. The same rules apply that you must generate genuine value and find a way to monetise it. Then the more you grow the enterprise, the more positive impact you can have.

Manage your money like a millionaire

A client going through career change once said to me, "I wish I could just have a million pounds sitting in my account so I didn't have to think about money any more." The problem is that even if you had a million pounds, if you spent a million and a half you'd still be broke (as many lottery winners have found out). There is never a point when you don't have to think about money and manage it well. Learn the habit now. You're unlikely to reach that million without it. There are now some excellent books and courses that make the whole topic, believe it or not, fun.

Start your play fund

One good discipline is to split your income and allocate it to different accounts for different purposes. Put aside a percentage for long-term saving. You might also choose to give 5–10% to a charity or cause of your choice. You then have the pleasure of knowing that as your income increases, so does your contribution. As an example, I donate 10% of the royalties from this book to War Child UK, which protects children in war zones.

Don't forget money for fun. Put aside 10% for your play fund. This is a savings fund for your play project and for anything else that feels fun and playful. Use your play fund to save up for a significant purchase for your play project: professional headshots, a photo editing app or a course to further your latest interest. Also use your play fund to treat yourself occasionally: pay for a fancy night out or other treat whenever you hit a release date for a project. It's a kind thing to do for yourself and primes your subconscious to know there is a pay-off when you've gone all out to get a project done.

When I had my first article published in a national newspaper, I took the whole payment out of the bank as cash and blew it on what was then the very latest portable music player. It seemed extravagant at the time but I ended up carrying it with me everywhere. And every time I looked at it, I remembered that it was my own creativity and initiative that had paid for it.

Is all this talk of spending money on indulging yourself pressing your buttons yet? Good. Read on.

Remove your internal blocks to getting rich

Have you noticed how some people always seem to have money throughout their lives and other people with similar talents and opportunities are always broke? Where are you on this scale?

What's your pattern? Have you always struggled? Or always managed to just get by? Or have you usually done well for yourself?

If money has often been a problem for you, or if you're doing OK but can't see how to do much better, it may be because you have some negative beliefs about money and what it would mean to be rich. If you think selling is tacky, marketing is conning people, rich people are all selfish, or charging a good price is ripping people off, it will be very difficult to get paid well for what you do.

I worked with a client once who had never earned very much money despite having a lot of talent, some great ideas and a certain level of fame. Sitting in my garden, I asked her what she thought of rich people. She burst out laughing and had to admit she immediately thought of all the worst possible icons of wealth: the selfish cigar-smoking tycoon, the entrepreneur that tramples on everyone else to get ahead. The problem with this is that it's very difficult to become something you despise. I asked her instead to think of three financially successful people that she actually respected. It took her a while but she came up with three great role models. I set her the homework to find images of these people online and place them somewhere she'll see them when she's working. This is a great exercise for anyone to do. Who would your three people be? Think of them as your virtual mentors.

Our beliefs and habits around money have a huge amount of influence on where we sit on the financial scale. If you pride yourself on not being concerned about money, you probably won't have any. Remember that money makes play sustainable. There are no prizes for being a starving artist or entrepreneur. If you feel comfortable earning a modest income and then start to earn more, you might subconsciously sabotage yourself to bring yourself back to what feels normal. And what feels normal is strongly influenced by your social group.

You are the average of the five people you spend the most time with.

Jim Rohn, American entrepreneur, author and speaker

Here's a little experiment. Add up the income of the five people you spend the most time with. Divide it by five to get the average. It's typical to find that your income is pretty close to this number. We saw in Secret four 'How to guarantee your success' how we are hypnotised by the thoughts, habits and beliefs we are surrounded by every day so it's not surprising that our closest friends will have an influence on our mindset and our expectations of life.

Imagine you spend all your time with people who earn half what you do. Your current income might start to feel pretty rich. In fact, you might begin to feel a bit uncomfortable around your friends, even a little guilty. Now imagine you are transported to another social circle where you spend all your time with people who earn at least twice what you currently do. You might start to feel a little embarrassed about your income and start to wonder if you could use some of the techniques your peers have used to get where they are. Can you see how these two very different experiences might influence your financial expectations and even your actions regarding money?

People who have created unusual levels of wealth of their own have different strategies and habits from ours, and these are bound to rub off on you over time. If you are serious about getting paid to play (and paid well), think about augmenting your social circle with some people who share your new values and might encourage some different approaches to wealth. This is particularly important if you currently inhabit a culture often found in the arts or non-profit world where people regularly struggle for funding (and may also have a negative view of people who don't).

Dare to charge what you're worth

It's impossible to get rich if you're not willing to charge well for (or otherwise monetise) the value you provide. Negotiating compensation for your work can be challenging, particularly if what you're selling is your own expertise or your creative output. If you have a habit of undercharging for what you do, take a tip from Pablo Picasso.

A Picasso original

According to the story, some decades ago a woman was strolling along a street in Paris when she spotted Picasso sketching at a sidewalk café. The woman asked Picasso if he would sketch her, and charge her accordingly. Picasso agreed. In just a few minutes, she had an original Picasso sketch of herself.

"And what do I owe you?" she asked. "Five thousand francs," he answered. "But it only took you three minutes!" she said. "No," Picasso said, "It took all my life."

Remember that our value to others is based on all that we bring – our natural talents, the skills we have developed and the experiences we have sought out. Think of everything you have invested in yourself and your business. Take out your playbook and add it all up – the training, the workshops, the costs of setting up your business. Include anything that you know you draw upon in your work. This is not just formal training. If your round-the-world trip taught you a heap of stuff about people, budgeting and organisation, put it on the list. Add a figure for all the years you lived on less than you would have liked because you were building something new.

Now, does what you're currently charging reflect this value? If not, start to think how you can charge according to the value you provide, not just the time you put in. You might find you attract better clients or customers. Undervaluing yourself tends to attract clients who undervalue you. Being too cheap sometimes puts good people off you altogether.

Would you like to get rich quick?

To get paid to play, you need to know how to play with capitalism. Capitalism may have its problems but for the time being it's here to stay so you might as well make friends with it. Interacting with your market is part of the game of being a player.

One of the fundamental models that underpins a free market is that of 'supply and demand'. I'm sure you've heard of it and yet many of us seem to forget all about it when it comes to earning a living off our own back.

What it means for you is that two things contribute to making more money from your playing: a smaller number of people who can supply what you do, or a larger number of people with a demand for it. Choosing your projects to alter either side of this equation in your favour will bring you a better return – provide something in short supply and choose things in great or rising demand.

Supply and demand also explains why there is no real way to get rich quickly. If there were an easy way to do something valuable and make you money, lots of people would rush to do it. Once that happened, the product would no longer be valuable because there would be an oversupply. When it was first realised that you could make money by sourcing a generic product from China (such as a kitchen utensil) and selling it on Amazon using their FBA service (Fulfilled By Amazon – which ships the product directly to the buyer without you touching it), lots of people starting doing it. This inevitably made the process much more competitive and therefore more difficult to succeed at. It is still possible to make money from Amazon FBA (I know people that do), but just like any business, the greatest rewards go to those who naturally suit the task of online marketing and are willing to learn everything needed to excel at it.

The exception to this rule is that there are occasionally critical moments in every industry when opportunities open up.

Regulation changes, new technology appears or a market reaches a tipping point. If you are ready to seize these moments when they appear, you can make money very quickly. To take advantage early before the bandwagon begins, you need to already be operating in that area and have the expertise to recognise the opportunity and make use of it.

By the time you see someone writing a book or running a workshop on how to make a quick buck from a new opportunity, you can be sure that the market will be far more competitive. That doesn't mean you shouldn't go near it. If getting into this area would be fun for you, your enthusiasm should support you in developing the skills you'll need to stand out from the 'me toos'. And whenever you're out there playing with a project, always keep an eye open for the moments when good opportunities appear.

How to get (a little more) rich quick

There may be no easy formula to become a millionaire overnight, but there are some simple ways to make yourself a little richer right away. Charge more for what you do by following my PRICE strategy. Some of my clients have doubled or even quadrupled their prices using this system.

P is for Product

Sell the right thing. The right thing is what there is a strong demand for (even if in a niche market), particularly something that solves a significant problem for people. Generally speaking, the bigger the problem you solve and the more people that have it, the easier it is to make money from it. You can also quickly increase what you typically make from each customer by bundling products and services into a package.

If you have specialist skills you enjoy using, this can help tip supply and demand in your favour. Invest in getting really good at what you do. When you find something you enjoy doing and have good skills for, don't be afraid to specialise in it. Then it's easier for people to understand what you offer and spread the word. Imagine you had lower back pain: who would you try first, a normal osteopath or a specialist lower back pain clinic if there were such a thing near you?

POWER-UP: Productise yourself for greater profit

If what you're offering is your own skills and expertise, you will often find you can sell more easily and actually charge more by 'productising' yourself. That means instead of billing yourself as a freelancer, therapist, coach or consultant, you create a unique offer and sell that. Think of a pressing need a particular market has and design a package, programme, course or workshop to address it. One of the advantages of doing this is that when you offer something that clearly says what you'll get out of it, it's easier for people to make the decision to buy it.

For example, instead of offering yourself as a hypnotherapist by the hour, create a comprehensive stop smoking plan that guarantees a result by the end of six weeks and when people see that it costs $1,000 they may well decide that it is worth that figure to them to become a non-smoker.

R is for the Right people

You can have the best product in the world but if the market you're approaching can't afford it, you won't make much money. Corporations, for example, can afford to pay much more than the general public for what you offer because what you do might benefit many staff or customers and the cost is spread across the whole business. If what you're offering is too expensive for your ideal client, find a different way to deliver it that makes it cheaper but allows you to provide it to more people. Can you turn your one-to-one service into a group programme you run online using the strategies in Secret seven?

I is for Increasing trust

It's much easier to sell what you offer if you can build trust and reduce the perceived risk for the buyer. Focus on creating a good track record and communicate it by encouraging word of mouth and using what's referred to as 'social proof' such as testimonials and case studies.

Be sure to include any relevant accolades on your website such as years of experience, qualifications, press coverage, well-known clients (if you are OK to name them), collaborations with more established people and organisations. This is not the time to be modest. You have to remember that someone coming to your website for the first time might have no knowledge of you at all and will be trying to decide whether to trust you.

A guarantee can dramatically reduce the perceived risk for your buyers. Offering a no-questions-asked, money-back guarantee on your product or service often makes far more in additional sales than what you might lose from the odd person taking advantage of it.

C is for Communicating value

Learn how to effectively communicate the value of what you do and stand by it. Don't apologise for charging a high price. Draw people in by identifying the problem you solve, then explain the benefits they will get and how much better their situation will be after they have used you or your product. If you're selling your expertise, price yourself on results not on time. Early on in my consulting career I once charged over a thousand pounds for a one-hour phone call and had no complaints because I was sharing my specialist expertise on a critical decision.

E is for Expect it and ask for it

The biggest reason I have managed to get paid so well for many of the things I have done, whether it's doubling my contract rate or getting £1,300 for my first magazine article 20 years ago, is that I simply dared to ask. It helps here to be clear on why you want it and deserve it. If you're worried you'll lose customers by putting up prices, try the new higher price on a special product or just on new customers. If you're good, you might be surprised just what people are willing to pay. And if it encourages you to raise the quality of your work even further, that's no bad thing.

If you're worried you'll price yourself out of your market, look for someone else that is charging a good price in your field. How do they do it? What can you use from them? Often the answer is to redefine yourself so that you are no longer compared with lower-priced competitors. If you're a web designer that also knows a lot about branding, relaunch as a brand designer and shake off the run-of-the-mill web design competition. You could run a group workshop to help people clarify their brand and then offer the attendees a special deal to implement their new brand on their websites.

What to do when someone says they can't afford it

You may find this hard to believe but it's never about the money. If someone says they can't afford it what they mean is they can't see the value yet. As long as you're selling to the right person then you simply haven't communicated the value well enough yet.

Would you have paid £5,000 for this book? Probably not. What if the book was the only copy specially written by Richard Branson and contained his secret guaranteed formula to make you a millionaire in 12 months? Perhaps you would – even if you had to sell your car (or a kidney) to get it. It's not the price that's the problem.

Beginning entrepreneurs often drop their prices when they have problems selling what they offer – and then are disappointed to find even that doesn't work well. If you are right at the beginning and looking to get more experience you might well give an early client a discount to close the deal. But once you're more experienced, instead of dropping your prices work to improve your skills in copywriting and sales.

Ultimately, if you've effectively communicated how you can solve someone's problem and they're still not going to buy, there is nothing you can do. Just move on to the next person. Some people will never spend the extra for good quality.

Choose a rich strategy

Remember, the best way to make a living is to provide genuine value to the world. If you're doing this then getting rich will mean providing more value to more people. If you want to make a million you have to provide a million of value. When you get there, you will have benefited others as much as yourself. I get annoyed when I see people providing great value to a tiny number of people but struggling financially because they've failed to ever expand their reach. They have never created a strategy to scale up or have never dared to play the fame game and get noticed. This is everyone's loss.

As we've seen earlier, it's difficult to get really rich selling your time or making your own handmade products, as there are only so many hours in the day. Ultimately you need something that can scale beyond what you can do on your own. You need a business. Your role then moves from working in delivering the product or service to working *on* your business.

If you're up for a challenge, one way to the rich life is to solve hard problems, whether that's creating the world's first healthy ice cream as the Oppo brothers did or building a good replacement for email which Slack did. What difficult problem do you feel strongly about and would enjoy playing with? What might engage your interest long enough to make a real impact on it? Making a success of it is likely to take you some considerable time and effort, so choosing something that you'll enjoy along the way is essential.

POWER-UP: Multiply yourself for greater impact and larger rewards

If you're already doing well in your current business ask yourself how you can provide that value to a lot more people. There are two primary ways to take something you provide personally and make it available to many more people – and that's using technology or people.

Scaling with technology

Can you bottle your knowledge, expertise, or service in the form of online courses people can take under their own steam as Taylor and Camille did with their PowerPoint knowledge? Or as an app like David with his smoke-free mobile app? This is an option that could suit you if you have existing technical or digital marketing skills. Or you are willing to hire someone that does.

Scaling with people

If you've developed a workshop, in-person programme or methodology that is having a positive impact on people, you could train people to deliver it for you. This could be the natural option for you if you're good at finding the right people and working to develop them.

Entrepreneurs Sophie and Audrey Boss have used a combination of both methods to scale their business Beyond Chocolate.

Sophie Boss of Beyond Chocolate grew her business with 'Chocolate Fairies'

When my sister Audrey and I started beyond chocolate we were running small-scale courses with women to improve their relationship with food so that they could stop dieting and end the obsession with food and their weight. Back then we were doing everything ourselves.

Then we wrote a book which generated far more demand than we could meet with our own in-person workshops, so we launched an online course. I had always said, "You can't do this online. Absolutely not. It's got to be personal. How can you possibly offer women the support they need through that medium?" But we found a way to do it that works! And that was by training what we originally called 'Chocolate Fairies' who are on the other end of the computer and respond to emails personally within 48 hours.

The course and the books still sell well but require practically none of our time and largely manage themselves. We have a wonderful closed Facebook group for all members which is moderated and managed by six of our trained facilitators from the early days. They do this without any need for financial reward – they get as much out of it as they put in. If they need to they can contact us to ask questions about tricky situations but it's rare. Mostly we keep in touch with them in the private team Facebook group.

All of this means that we are now freed for other things including running Beyond Chocolate residential retreats on our land in Puglia, Italy. We run three or four of them a year and they are so satisfying to run – and profitable.

Read more about Beyond Chocolate at www.beyondchocolate.co.uk

Think about how you could collaborate with others to help you scale up. Once you can offer something people really want without having to deliver it yourself, look for connections with others that can quickly multiply your business. Just one good retailer or agent or joint venture partner can transform the money you're making by supplying what you do to a whole new market. And if you follow the process laid out so far in the book they might come and find you before you even go looking.

Start crafting your rich strategy today. Learn from the stories of others in your field to find out how they scaled up to create a business out of their first experiments. If you're determined enough, you can join them in playing your way to your own version of the rich life.

Put it into play

Keys to this secret:

➡ Describe your vision of the rich life and be creative about how you can get some of the experience now.
➡ Manage your money like a millionaire and start your play fund.
➡ Work on your internal blocks to getting rich.
➡ Use the PRICE strategy to charge what you're worth.
➡ Create a rich strategy with something that scales.

What you should have now:

➡ A strategy to maximise the return on your playing and enjoy the process.

Take ten minutes to play:

➡ Set up an account for your play fund.
➡ Brainstorm a way to have a small experience of your rich life now.
➡ Sketch out some ways to create your rich strategy in your playbook.

Exclusive extras on fworkletsplay.com:

➡ Listen to interviews with successful entrepreneurs who have scaled their businesses to remarkable heights.

➡ Access links to learn more about managing money and creating a portable business to support your travels, and find details of programmes from The Ideas Lab on starting and scaling your own business.

Let's play

Let's make this really clear, you can always have the experience you really want in your work as long as you're flexible about the form it will come in. You can start right now, and you are *guaranteed* to get it if you simply *do not stop*.

As long as you're in the wrong work or failing to make the most of your talents, you're short-changing not just yourself but the world. As I said to a client recently who was stuck prevaricating about what to do next, "You know, it's not all about you. Stop obsessing about what to do and whether you can do it and just start doing it – because I'd like to see some of these interesting ideas of yours actually happen."

We're waiting for you to do your thing. If you haven't taken action yet, it's time to start. Pick a play project that will last 30 days or less and that will take you one step closer to getting paid to do what you love. Grab your playbook (or the nearest scrap of paper), write a list of five things that will get you started. Each should take no more than half an hour, maybe less. Choose one you can do right now. Put the book down. Go do it. Notice the results you get and adjust your direction accordingly. Choose your next task and put an appointment in your diary to do that. Repeat. Don't stop.

Let's play. I believe it's your turn.

Let me know how you get on via Twitter at @johnsw

Bonus content

fworkletsplay.com, the accompanying website for this book, contains a whole heap of exclusive additional content to help you get paid to play:

- ➡ Download editable worksheets for you to choose the right business idea for you.

- ➡ Read, listen to and watch full interviews with successful players, from people just starting out to multi-millionaires.

- ➡ More information and website links for every topic covered in each chapter of the book.

- ➡ Connect with a global online community of players.

- ➡ More information on events and programmes at The Ideas Lab to help you create and launch a stand-out business, including the free 5-Day Business Startup Challenge.

- ➡ Get my up to date list of favourite online tools for starting and marketing your business on a shoestring including websites, hosting, email marketing and more.

- ➡ My free web-class on how to create a business or career that becomes #1 in your market.

- ➡ Examples of successful campaigns people have run to win their first playcheque.

- ➡ Links to up-to-date resources to learn more about managing money, creating a portable business to support your travels, and workshops on the mindset of wealth.

- ➡ Details of how to contact me via email and social media.

Go to fworkletsplay.com now and dive in.

About War Child UK

Ten per cent of ongoing author royalties for this book will be donated to War Child UK, the international charity that protects children living in the world's most dangerous war zones including Iraq, Afghanistan, the Democratic Republic of Congo, Uganda and Syria.

War Child UK protects children from the brutal effects of war and its consequences. Its work with former child soldiers, children in prison and children living and working on the streets gives them support, protection and opportunities.

War Child UK's staff are on the ground helping thousands of kids to rebuild their lives. By working with local partners, they provide a number of services for children including:

➡ rebuilding schools destroyed by war and getting children back into education

➡ separating children from adult detainees in prison and providing legal aid

➡ reintegrating child soldiers with their families

➡ getting children off the streets after war has forced them to leave home

➡ vocational and professional training which gives them future opportunities

➡ ensuring children get access to food

➡ counselling to help children cope with their trauma, to build friendships and to learn to play again.

War Child UK makes creative use of music in its work to raise funds with its superb live events featuring famous names, and in its work with the children themselves. When War Child first went to Bosnia, music therapy was one of the tools they used to help kids come to terms with their traumatic experiences. And in Kinshasa in the Democratic Republic of Congo, War Child UK hosted a rap battle for the street kids it works with. It also took some of them into a studio with a Congolese rap artist to record a track about their lives and their dreams for the future.

To read more about War Child or to make a donation, go to www.warchild.org.uk

The 21 myths of work

Index